THE YOM KIPPUR WAR:
A Case Study in Crisis Decision-Making in American Foreign Policy

Ray Maghroori
Department of Political Science
University of California
Riverside, California

Stephen M. Gorman
Department of Political Science
North Texas State University
Denton, Texas

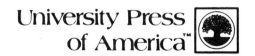
University Press
of America™

Library of Congress Cataloging in Publication Data

Maghroori, Ray.
    The Yom Kippur War.

    Bibliography: p.
    1. Israel-Arab War, 1973--Diplomatic history.
2. United States--Foreign relations--Near East.
3. Near East--Foreign relations--United States.
4. United States--Foreign relations--1969-1974.
I. Gorman, Stephen M., joint author. II. Title.
DS128.12.M34 1981   956'.048   80-5811
ISBN 0-8191-1373-5
ISBN 0-8191-1374-3 (pbk.)

ACKNOWLEDGEMENTS

e would like to thank Rebecca Swartz and Penny
andley for their assistance in preparing the
nal manuscript.

iii

iv

CONTENTS

Introduction

The 1973 October War between the Israelis and Arabs can be considered a watershed in American foreign policy in the Middle East. The conflict brought about a myriad of political, economic and even psychological changes both within the international environment and within the American and Israeli domestic settings. The single most significant economic impact of the war was the emergence of oil as a political-diplomatic weapon which provided the Arab world with a new influence in global affairs, and a specific source of leverage in the search for a comprehensive resolution of the Middle East conflict. Among the political transformations brought about by the war, the new balance of military force in the region had the greatest impact. The Arabs fought better and with more determination and discipline than the Israelis had thought them capable. And although, the Arabs did not achieve an unqualified military victory in 1973, many observers began to suspect that in future confrontations an Arab victory would become increasingly conceivable. This led in turn to an important psychological shift in Israel away from a one sided reliance on military might for security to a gradually expanding search for lasting political solutions.

The October War had direct and far reaching consequences for the United States because of Washington's close association with the Jewish State. The rise of Arab economic, political and military power affected American interests in a number of ways. First, the oil embargo forced many Americans to realize that direct military support for the Israelis would no longer be cost-free, and they therefore began to pay more critical attention to the policies of the American government toward the Arab world. Second, American assistance to Israel during the war weakened American cooperation with Western Europe and Japan which, because they imported more of their oil from the Middle East than the United States, were more severely affected by the Arab oil embargo. Washington was forced to consider the trade-offs between continued one-sided support for the Israelis and the likely effects of another Middle Eastern confrontation on American interests elsewhere in the world. Many traditional American allies began to disassociate themselves from Washington's Middle Eastern policy in order to escape future Arab economic retaliations. Finally, the October War revealed how easily a conflict in the Middle East could escalate into a confrontation between the United States and the Soviet Union. Hence, the Arab-Israeli dispute could no longer be viewed as a purely localized problem with little immediate consequence for global peace and security.

American foreign policy in the Middle East during the period surrounding the October War is not only interesting because of the lasting importance of the events that unfolded, but also because of the nature of the processes by which policy decisions were made. There are a number of questions that remain about the adequacy of the perceptions of American foreign policy-makers and the reliability of their motivations for pursuing different policy options. For example, available evidence suggests that the United States missed an important opportunity to prevent the outbreak of the October War as a result of the narrow and rigid assumptions of foreign policy makers. When Egypt expelled Soviet advisors in 1972 and communicated its willingness to work with the United States in breaking the stalemate in the region, Washington failed to take the initiative in pressing for a peaceful settlement to the conflict. American assessments of Arab intentions and capabilities led to the conclusion that there was no immediate danger of armed conflict, and therefore no pressing need to adjust

2

American policies to head-off war. The intransigence of American Middle Eastern policy leading up to the October War raises the question whether officials in Washington are flexible enough to respond quickly and effectively to new developments or whether they become prisoners of outmoded cognitive frameworks that can only be shaken by the appearance of major crises. The issue is whether policy-makers understand and move with events, or merely react to events which they were unable to anticipate because of what might be called "grooved thinking." The American experience in the October War points to the second conclusion.

Washington's conduct during the course of the war is equally significant since it provides insight into how decisions are made in a crisis situation and the range of possible motivations that can produce any given policy. Two American actions decided on during the course of the war deserve attention. The first was the American military airlift to Israel, second the American global military alert in response to a possible Soviet military intervention in the Sinai. Both policies appear puzzling from the standpoint of their objectives and the motivations behind them. For instance, did the United States decide to supply Israel with military equipment as a response to the Soviet military airlift to Egypt, because Israel was in danger of losing the war or out of fear that Israel's supporters in Congress would attack the Nixon administration for its lack of active assistance to the Jewish state? Or, for example, was the American nuclear alert a response to a real danger of Soviet military intervention in the Middle East or simply a convenient device for distracting American public attention away from President Nixon's political problems connected with Watergate?

Lastly, aside from providing insight into the way in which American foreign policy is made, a study of the United States' involvement in the October War can serve as an important case study

of Henry Kissinger's approach to international
relations. Kissinger emerges from a study of the
October War as the dominant figure. Acting almost
in complete isolation from the foreign policy
making establishment and from the Congress, and
with extensive freedom of action granted him by a
President preoccupied with a partisan domestic
political challenge, Kissinger forged the American
response to the Arab-Israeli conflict almost
single handedly. American policies during the
war would therefore seem to provide the clearest
test of Kissinger's skills as a statesman. Yet,
in practice his behavior is difficult to assess
and his motives nearly impossible to discern.
If anything, Kissinger emerges from a study of
the October War as an even greater enigma than
before. But the undertaking is nevertheless useful
since his role in coordinating America's response
to events in the Middle East between 1973-74
reveals certain characteristics of his diplomatic
style and demonstrates the excessive impact that
one man can have on the course of global events--
even in an age of bureaucratic decision-making.

The following discussion will be divided
between a review of the events leading up to the
October War, the forces behind the American
decision to airlift military supplies to Israel
during the course of the war, the negotiations
leading to the cease-fire agreements terminating
hostilities and, finally, the decision to place
American armed forces on global alert. After
reviewing American actions in the Middle East in
the period surrounding the October War we will
then be in a position to offer certain tentative
generalizations about the decision-making process
in American foreign policy.

Soviet Departure from Egypt

A consistent pattern in the American approach
to world affairs is the lack of flexibility to
adapt to changing environments. Rigid ideological

4

and bureaucratic preconceptions often impede adjustments in policy. As a result, American foreign policy is often out of phase with the existing realities of the external environment. In their quest for preserving the stability of the foreign policy system, American statesmen often fail to act before sudden disturbances in the international arena impose a sense of urgency. It is only then that adjustments are made and new policies are formulated. American Middle Eastern policy is an excellent demonstration of this problem. There were several important developments in the Middle East during the early 1970s which in retrospect appear to have been developments that, had they been responded to purposefully, could have promoted American interest in the region. One such development was the rift between the Soviet Union and Egypt, reflected in Cairo's decision to expel Soviet advisors from Egypt in the summer of 1972.[1]

The reason behind the Egyptian decision is complex, but reflected President Sadat's distrust of Moscow's objectives in the region. In 1971, Ali Sabri, a pro-Soviet, high ranking Egyptian, tried unsuccessfully to oust Sadat.[2] This attempted coup d'etat failed and Sabri and his supporters were jailed. Sadat suspected Soviet complicity, but because of Egypt's military dependence on the Soviet Union he decided to let the issue fade away. However, he never dismissed the possibility that the Soviets might try to replace him with a more pro-Soviet leader. Recent events in Afghanistan seem to support Sadat's assessment that the Soviets were capable of overthrowing less than compliant allies. This factor contributed substantially to Sadat's expulsion of the Soviets from Egypt, but there were other important considerations as well. There was considerable concern in Egypt, for example, over the presence of Soviet advisors. In the context of the Brezhnev doctrine, which justified Soviet intervention in the domestic affairs of other socialist countries, some Egyptians "feared that if friction developed with the Soviets, they might repeat their Czechoslovak tactics: after all, they had their technicians and their own airport and could bring as many of their troops into Egypt as they wanted."[3]

While these two factors were important, it was a third element that triggered the decision. Throughout 1971 and early 1972, Sadat had tried without success to obtain offensive weapons from Moscow. In June 1972, after the first Nixon summit visit to the Soviet Union, Sadat tried once more to gain Soviet arms and support for a military campaign against Israel. But in the context of Soviet détente with the United States, Moscow seemed uncooperative. The Soviets refused the Egyptian request for military hardware made by Sadat's Minister of War, General Mohammed Ahmed Sadiq, when he visited Moscow on 7 June 1972.[4] A further attempt was made in mid-July. Hoping that he could still extract some concessions from Moscow, Sadat dispatched his Prime Minister, Aziz Sidiq, and his Foreign Minister, Murad Ghaleb, to Moscow on 13 July. They were scheduled to stay for three days, but returned after only one. The day after Sidiq's return from Moscow, the exodus of Soviet military personnel began - although Sadat's decision did not become public until a few days later.[5] The Egyptian leader, on 24 July, gave his own explanation for the expulsion of the Soviets. According to Sadat:

> I told the Soviet leaders there were three issues we would not accept. I drew their attention to the fact that they should not agree to any restrictions on arms deliveries before the consequences of the aggression had been removed, otherwise Israel would remain superior and the Arabs would lag behind. The second issue was the continued state of no peace and no war in the area, which we also would not tolerate. The third issue was the Arab countries' borders; I asked that the Soviets should not be

dragged into a discussion of any
Arab surrender of even one inch of
Arab land.[6]

Furthermore, Sadat was concerned about the
Soviet-American détente and its consequence for
Moscow's relations with Egypt. He feared that
the Soviet desire to improve relations with the
Americans might cause a reduction in the Soviet
commitment to the Arabs. This fear became
accentuated when the Egyptians learned that the
Middle East issue had not been adopted as a
subject of serious negotiations during the Soviet-
American summit in May 1972. Thus, by July
Sadat had become convinced that "Moscow had
relegated the Middle East to a low place on the
international agenda, and at Egypt's expense."[7]

Although there is no direct evidence, it is
conceivable that Sadat's decision also reflected
a desire to move closer to the United States.[8]
Indeed, Sadat had mentioned the possibility of
expelling the Soviets to a group of American
Congressmen when they visited Cairo in May 1971.
Referring to his interview with Sadat, Representative Clarence D. Long told a Congressional
hearing that:

> He (Sadat) went on further to inti-
> mate a desire to get the Russians
> out. In his words, 'I want to be
> frank with you. I am very grateful
> to the Russians; they helped us in
> our hour of need and I am going to
> give them bases, but I went to jail
> to get rid of the British and I
> don't want any foreigners on my
> soil.'[9]

Yet despite this early signal, the departure of
the Soviets from Egypt took many American
officials by surprise.

The expulsion of Soviet advisors from Egypt
created a political vacuum in the Middle East.

7

It posed a unique opportunity for the United States to increase its influence in the Arab world. Furthermore, by pressuring Israel into some concessions, the United States might even have defused the Arab-Israel conflict and thereby have prevented the outbreak of the October War in 1973. However, 1972 was a presidential election year, and Nixon could not risk the repercussions of a sudden change in the direction of the American Middle Eastern policy. According to Lawrence L. Whetten:

> The United States had insisted that the expulsion of the Soviet military forces from Egypt was a precondition for a durable settlement. When this was achieved by Arab, rather than American action, Washington was unable to move decisively to introduce fluidity into the local player's position. . . . With the Soviets in seeming disgrace, only the Americans could have moved the confrontation toward settlement. But the apathy resulting from repeated Israeli vetoes of American good intentions and constraints arising from the forthcoming presidential campaign precluded any American initiative at that time.[10]

Even after the 1972 elections, and after Nixon's landslide victory, the Nixon-Kissinger team seemed reluctant to take the initiative in the Middle East. In February 1973, hoping that Nixon's re-election might have removed the domestic constraints on the Republican Administration, Sadat dispatched his advisor on National Security Affairs, Hafez Ismail, to Washington. Ismail met with both Nixon and Kissinger,[11] but the Egyptian envoy failed to convince the Americans that there was any pressing need for a new approach to the Middle East conflict. Apparently, even after the expulsion of the Soviet advisors Kissinger did not feel that the time had come for him to act.

8

Despite his intellectual dislike for policies that
were made "through a series of more or less vio-
lent and frequently catastrophic upheavals,"[12]
Kissinger - as a statesman - decided to wait for
a crisis, because, as he told friends, "I can't
do anything until I have all the strings in my
hand, and I won't have them in my hand until
there is a crisis."[13]   Thus, while Ismail's talks
with the American officials were described as
"warm, objective, and fruitful," they did little
to alter the Arab-Israeli conflict and the position of the United States in the Middle East.[14]

The War

It is now clear that the preparation for the
October War began before Nassar's death and before
the War of Attrition.[15]   But, prior to Spring
1973 there was still some hope of a diplomatic
solution. Despite his early hard line approach,
Sadat was willing to use diplomacy in place of
war. Indeed, by the time of Ismail's visit to
Washington, "Sadat was prepared to consider any
terms, except direct talks."[16]   Yet, not only did
the Americans seem reluctant to exert pressure
on Israel at this time, but also, a few days
after Ismail's visit, the United States announced
that it was going to supply Israel with forty-
eight additional Phantoms.[17]   It was this announcement that caused Sadat to abandon all hope of
breaking the deadlock by political means.[18]
Shortly after Ismail's return to Cairo, Sadat
announced to the national assembly on 26 March
that he was taking over the premiership in order
to strengthen the war effort. In his message to
the assembly he declared that:

> The state of total confrontation
> has become inevitable, and we are
> entering it whether we like it or
> not. The military situation must
> be made to move, with all the
> sacrifices that this entails. We

9

must tell the world that we are
here and that we can dictate our
will.[19]

Throughout 1971 and 1972, Sadat had talked about
"the year of decision" and inevitable war with
the enemy.[20]   But this time Sadat was not
bluffing: in a few months, the Egyptian troops
would cross the Suez Canal.

The fourth major clash between the Arabs
and the Israelis erupted on 6 October 1973. On
the day of Yom Kippur, in a well-coordinated
military operation, the Egyptian and Syrian forces
attacked the Israelis along the Suez Canal and
the Golan Heights, respectively.[21]   Within a few
hours after the fighting began, Egyptian forces,
supported by intensive fire from Egyptian-manned
SAM-2 and SAM-3 missiles, crossed the Suez Canal
at five points. By the end of the day, they
destroyed the Israeli defense line on the east
bank. By 7 October, some four hundred Egyptian
tanks crossed Egyptian pontoon bridges and
marched eastward. On 8 October, Cairo announced
that the Egyptian troops were in control of the
entire east bank. On 14 October, the Egyptians
launched a new offensive from the east bank
toward the strategic Mitla Pass but encountered
severe Israeli resistance, and both sides suffered
heavy casualties.

The slowdown in the Egyptian offensive provided Israel with an opportunity to counter-
attack. On 16 October, an Israeli task force
succeeded in crossing the canal. Subsequently,
the Israelis developed their thrust, and by 19
October, Israel had some ten thousand men and two
hundred tanks on the west bank. When fighting
came to an end in late October, the Israelis had
pushed some fifteen miles into Egypt and were in
control of 1,200 square kilometers of the west
bank of the Suez Canal.[22]   By crossing the canal,
the Israeli army was able to encircle the
Egyptian third army on the east bank. Some

twenty thousand Egyptian troops on the Sinai were
at Israel's mercy for their supplies of food and
water.

In the northern front, the Israelis and the
Syrians fought a bloody war. Initially, the
Syrians advanced over fifteen miles into Israeli-
held territory along the Golan Heights. But by
10 October the Israelis, who had concentrated
their forces on the Syrian front, were able to
recapture the entire Golan Heights. By 11 October,
the Syrians were driven back beyond the cease-
fire lines; and by 12 October the Israeli forces
were only twenty miles from Damascus.

The fighting came to an end on 22 October
when, as a result of intensive private negotiations, the US and the USSR agreed on the text of
a Security Council Resolution calling on the
belligerents "to cease all firing and terminate
all military activity."[23] Despite the acceptance of the UN resolution by all parties, some
fighting continued after the cease-fire went
into effect. It was only after the Security
Council had adopted two further resolutions, on
23 and 25 October, that the October War finally
came to a complete halt.[24] Although relatively
brief in duration, the October War was extremely
costly in terms of both men and equipment.
Total casualties amounted to 88,331, and over
twenty-one hundred tanks and nearly five hundred
aircraft were lost.

American Foreign Policy During the War

The United States learned about the outbreak
of war a few hours after it began. Even as late
as 5 October, Kissinger, who had recently succeeded William Rogers as Secretary of State, "had
operated on the assumption that the situation in
the Middle East, while always volatile, was still
manageable."[25] Kissinger's beliefs were reinforced by the Israeli interpretation of the events

11

immediately preceding the war. As late as 4
October, the Israelis were convinced that troop
maneuvers detected by the CIA along the Golan
front were still "defensive in posture."[26] Thus,
the news of the war "took Kissinger completely by
surprise." Because there was an Arab terrorist
attack the preceding week against a group of Jews
in Vienna, the American Secretary of State even
thought that the war might have been initiated by
the Israelis in retaliation for Arab terrorism.[27]
But when he called the Israeli embassy and con-
sulted with Israeli officials, Kissinger was [28]
assured that the Arabs had initiated the war.

Some analysts have argued that Kissinger
knew about the Arab war plan as early as Spring
1973. It has been argued by Tad Szulc, for
example, that the American intelligence community
had obtained a copy of a "detailed three-phase
Egyptian attack plan" in April.[29] Furthermore,
according to Szulc, "The Soviet Ambassador,
Anatoloyi Dobrynin, advised Kissinger on 5 October
that the Arab offensive would be launched the
following day."[30] Szulc further argues that the
United States immediately informed the Israelis.

There is some evidence supporting the report
regarding American possession of the Egyptian
war plan. In April 1973, Arnaud de Borchgrave
of Newsweek interviewed Sadat in Cairo. In this
interview, Sadat sounded alarmed. He told de
Borchgrave that:

> Now the time has come for a deci-
> sion. . . the time has come for a
> shock. Diplomacy will continue
> before, during, and after the
> battle. . . . Everything in this
> country is now being mobilized in
> earnest for the resumption of the [31]
> battle — which is now inevitable. . .

According to some reports, Kissinger reacted to
Sadat's remarks by commenting that, "I expect [32]
something to happen which can be very serious."

It is doubtful that Kissinger's comment was
simply in reaction to Sadat's interview. Sadat
had made similar remarks on many occasions—beginning in 1971 when he began to talk about "the
year of decision." Therefore it is conceivable
the U.S. had access to information regarding the
Egyptian war plan which made Sadat's remarks
credible to Kissinger. There is a further piece
of evidence supporting Szulc's first argument.
In May, the Israeli reserves were partially
mobilized--indicating that the Israelis were
anticipating an attack. Of course, no attack
occurred and, therefore, the mobilization was
called off.[33]

As far as the second part of Szulc's argument is concerned--that the Soviets informed
Kissinger of an impending Arab attack on 5 Oct-
ober--the evidence does not seem compelling. Had
Kissinger known about the imminent outbreak of
war, he would most likly have returned to Washington after his day at the UN. He would not
have spent the night in New York as he actually
did. Besides, there are conflicting reports
regarding the Soviet involvement in the October
War.[34] Did Moscow know about the war? Sadat
has made contradictory remarks on the subject.
Early in 1974, he told de Borchgrave that the
Soviets were not informed of the Arab war plan.
A year and a half later, however, Sadat changed
his story. In a speech on 15 September 1975, he
revealed that the Soviets were informed about the
war on 3 October.[35] The difficult question is
why the Egyptians would have informed the Soviets
of their military intentions after expelling
Soviet advisors from their country. One plausible explanation is that by committing themselves
to an attack on Israel, the Egyptians could
place more pressure on Moscow to supply additional
military hardware. Another explanation is that
Sadat was attempting to communicate to the Soviets
in the strongest terms possible his unwillingness
to accept the existing stalemate, and thereby
place pressure on Moscow to use its influence to
push for a breakthrough in the Middle Eastern

13

situation. Finally, it is not unlikely that the Soviets learned of Egyptian war plans through their own information sources located in the Egyptian government. But even if the Soviets were aware of the approach of war, this is not to say that they necessarily gave their formal or informal approval to the Egyptian-Syrian war plan.

Some argue that the Arabs must have had a tacit Soviet approval (or else forced the Soviets to assist them by creating a confrontation). Not only was it the Soviet military hardware that made the war possible,[36] but also, as one analyst has argued, it is "doubtful that Sadat would ever have embarked on his dangerous course without Soviet assurance of resupply of military equipments if events made it necessary."[37] However, what is not clear yet is the question of the Soviets' advance knowledge of the date of the attack. According to Alvin Rubinstein, "By late September/early October the Soviets were fully aware of the imminence of war."[38] Rubinstein provides several bits of evidence in support of his argument. Probably the most important piece of information is that beginning on 3 October, Soviet dependents in Syria and Egypt were hastily evacuated, a fact which suggests that Moscow expected the war to begin within a few days.[39]

If we assume that the Soviets had known about the war, either directly or indirectly, would they have informed the Americans? Theoretically, there are at least two possibilities: 1) Moscow informs the US, assuming that the Americans will notify the Israelis; 2) Moscow informs the US, but it is assured that the Israelis are not informed. While the second alternative is a theoretical possibility, in the context of the close American-Israeli relations the possibility of this second scenario is so low that it does not require much serious consideration. Thus, let us consider only the first possibility.

It seems doubtful that the Russians would

have informed the Americans under the assumptions of the first scenario. To a great extent,
the initial success of the Arab military campaign in 1973 was due to the element of surprise.
Thus, if the Israelis had been informed, even
if they did not preempt for political reasons, [40]
the advanced warning would have provided them
with the opportunity to mobilize their reserves.
Under this circumstance, the Arabs would have
suffered another severe blow—similar to the one
in 1967. But how could the Soviets benefit
from such an outcome? A superpower cannot afford
two devastating defeats for its major military
client within six years. An Arab defeat would
not only reflect on Arab military strength, but
also on the level of sophistication of Soviet military technology. Would the Soviets have poured
billions of dollars worth of military hardware
into Egypt and Syria simply to allow the Israelis
to destroy it? The reputational costs of such a
policy make this doubtful.

It therefore seems unlikely that the Soviets
would have informed Washington of Arab military
intentions since they could gain little by such
an action. Of course the Soviets may have communicated certain danger signals to the United
States in order to demonstrate their own concern
over tensions in the area, thereby placing Moscow
in the position of having warned Washington of
the explosive situation in the Middle East. But
even if Moscow did not in some fashion inform
Washington of the prospects for war in the Middle
East, this is not to say that the United States
was therefore blameless for being caught by
surprise when the Arabs attacked Israel. No doubt
Washington was caught off-guard, as Kissinger
himself has stated. Nevertheless, American foreign policy experts created the conditions for
being caught off-guard by adopting rigid and
stereotypical attitudes toward the Arab world.
Accordingly, Washington was unable to understand
the significance of the political split between
Moscow and Cairo, could not appreciate the domestic political pressures that might force Arab

leaders into another war with Israel and, finally,
drastically underestimated Arab military capabilities.

In view of the dominant American attitudes
toward the Middle Eastern situation (i.e., that
Israel possessed the requisite power to maintain
the status quo and that the Arabs were therefore
unwilling to risk confrontation), it is interesting to consider the possibility that the
Russians did inform the United States of the
impending Arab attack on Israel. It is conceivable that, in the first instance, Moscow
interpreted the Egyptian war plan as a device to
extract more military equipment from the Soviet
Union, and not necessarily as a serious proposal.
The Soviets might then have informed Washington
of the Arab war plan, possibly to demonstrate
good faith (since Moscow may not have taken the
plan seriously) to promote US-Soviet cooperation
in other areas. At this point in the process,
the attitudes of American policy makers would
have become critical. Would the information have
been taken seriously, studies initiated and field
information generated to either confirm or dis-
prove the existence of an Arab military threat,
or would the information have been discarded
because it did not fit with the prevailing
assumptions about the Middle East? After all,
the Soviets may have implied by their own behavior
that an Arab attack had a low level of probability.
Finally, would Washington have warned Israel, and
how strong would the warning have been? The
Israelis, for their part, might have been just
as inclined to dismiss the notion of an Arab
military assault as the Americans, and much would
have depended on the intelligence reports that
accompanied the warning which, because of the
indirect nature of the information, would have
been scant. In short, the intelligence of an
Arab plan to attack Israel may in fact have been
passed from the Soviets to the Americans to the
Israelis, but at each step it was given less and
less credibility.

The October War was not simply a war between the Arabs and the Israelis, although only Arab and Israeli soldiers fought in the war. To a great extent the war was facilitated by the policies of the US and the USSR. It was the Soviet SAMs that made it possible for the Egyptians to cross the canal. And it was American Phantom jets that gave the Israelis the capability to conduct raids deep into Syria and Egypt. It can even be argued that without the massive Soviet military supplies to Egypt and Syria, the October War could not have been initiated.[41] And in the same regard, it might be argued that without American military aid to Israel during the war, "the conflict might have ended with an Arab military victory."[42] Therefore, the war also involved an indirect contest between Soviet and American arms.

There is a great deal of controversy concerning the role of Henry Kissinger in the formulation of the policy to supply the Israeli forces during the war. Basically, there are two contending views about Kissinger's role. According to one version, the Secretary was determined from the very beginning of the war to supply Israel's military needs.[43] Thus, on 7 October when the Israeli Ambassador to Washington asked for American military equipment, "Kissinger responded sympathetically to Dinitz's plea and promised to help."[44] However, according to this version, Secretary of Defense James Schlesinger refused to cooperate with Kissinger. On 8 October, Schlesinger "rejected a request that Israeli planes be allowed to land in the United States to pick up ammunition."[45] Apparently, the Secretary of Defense was concerned about the Arabs' reaction and its impact on American access to Middle Eastern oil. When Dinitz learned of Schlesinger's decision, the Israeli Ambassador appealed to Kissinger. After an exchange with the Pentagon, Kissinger called Dinitz to inform him that:

> Permission had been granted for a
> 'limited number of Israeli planes'
> to land at US bases and pick up

supplies, 'provided they paint
their tails,' that is, paint over
the identifying six-pointed Jewish
star.[46]

A few hours later, Kissinger called Dinitz again
to inform him that Nixon had agreed, in principle,
to replace Israeli plane losses.[47]

By 9 October, the Israelis had suffered
considerable casualties (they had lost twenty
percent of their air force) and were in need of
new military equipment. By 8:15 a.m., Dinitz
was in Kissinger's office repeating "his urgent
demand for planes and tanks."[48] Dinitz was disturbed by the fact that despite Kissinger's
promise to help two days earlier, Israel had not
yet received any supplies. Kissinger again
sounded sympathetic, and he told Dinitz that he
had difficulties with the bureaucracy, "implying
that he was engaged in a one-on-one fight with
the Pentagon to fulfill the Israeli request."[49]
To assure Dinitz of his cooperation and good intentions, he had a private hot line put into
Dinitz's office connecting the Israeli Embassy to
the State Department.

According to at least one account, Kissinger
conferred with Nixon on the afternoon of 9 October.
In the evening he called Dinitz and informed him
that:

The President had approved 'all'
the Israeli requests. All plane
and tank losses would be replaced.
All electronic equipment, including
jamming devices, would be furnished,
and Israeli transport planes would
be permitted to land at the Oceana
Naval Air Station at Virginia Beach,
Virginia . . .[50]

The next day, Dinitz again met with Kissinger
at the State Department. He informed the Secretary of State that the Soviets had begun an airlift

18

to Egypt and Syria and that to offset the Soviet
supplies the Israelis needed American military
hardware immediately. Kissinger agreed. According
to this account, he called Schlesinger asking him to
organize civilian charters to transfer the American supplies to Israel, but Schlesinger showed
little enthusiasm. Indeed, at the last minute the
Defense Secretary cancelled a noon-time meeting
with Dinitz set to discuss the details of the
American military transfer. Apparently, Schlesinger's deputy, William Clements, "a wealthy Texas
drilling contractor with close ties to the oil
industry," had convinced the secretary that "he
needed more information about American inventories
before he could provide the Israelis with an exact
timetable for the deliveries."[51] Dinitz was
furious. He met with Kissinger again in the
evening and registered his complaints.

The Israeli Ambassador was back in Kissinger's
office at 7:40 a.m. the next day. Again Kissinger seemed sympathetic. Indeed, he seemed very
determined to get the supplies to the Israelis.
Kissinger had received reports the day before
from the CIA that the Soviet airlift had become
"massive." Thus, he now came to view the issue
of supplying Israel with military equipment not
simply in terms of the survival of the Jewish
state, but also as a challenge in Soviet-American
relations: "To spare the world from the possibility of a big-power confrontation," he was determined "to open a massive airlift of American
supplies to Israel."[52] At the conclusion of his
meeting with Kissinger, Dinitz again was assured
that Israel's needs would be met quickly. The
secretary told Dinitz to contact Schlesinger who,
Kissinger implied, "would be more accommodating."[53]

A few hours later, Kissinger called Dinitz
at the Israeli Embassy. He told the ambassador
that he had spoken to Schlesinger about the
possibility of using civilian American airplanes
for the purpose of transferring arms to Israel.
Schlesinger had resisted the idea because he
feared an oil embargo. But Kissinger had talked

19

to Nixon, and the president had now ordered
Schlesinger to charter twenty transport planes.

By the next morning, Dinitz had still not
heard from the Defense Department. He called
Kissinger on his hot line to complain. Kissinger,
according to Marvin and Bernard Kalb, was angry.
He told the ambassador that he would check with
the Pentagon and would call him back. Kissinger
called Schlesinger and, "in the president's name,
instructed him to arrange for the charter of
twenty civilian transport planes."[54] The Secretary of Defense said that he had tried to hire
civilian charters, but failed. Most companies,
he explained, "did not want to get involved in
the Middle East war." "In that case," Kissinger
reportedly replied, "get military planes and get
them quickly."[55] At 10:30 that morning, Dinitz
received a call from the Pentagon informing him
that U.S. military planes would be used for
the purpose of transferring supplies to Israel.

Dinitz was back in Kissinger's office at
11:00 p.m. complaining again. He had met with
Schlesinger and his deputies earlier in the
evening and was told that the American military
planes would transport the goods only as far as
the Azore Islands and that Israel had to make
other arrangements to get the supplies from the
Azores to Tel Aviv. Moreover, Schlesinger had
informed Dinitz that the US would provide Israel
with only sixteen Phantom planes, although
Israel had asked for a minimum of thirty-two.
Kissinger again seemed cooperative and sympathetic.
He told Dinitz that he would do "everything in my
power" to overcome "bureaucratic difficulties."
Dinitz thanked Kissinger, but he also made it
clear to the Secretary of State that unless
Israel's needs were met promptly he would soon
"go public," implying that he would appeal to
Israel's supporters in Congress.[56]

Kissinger knew that Dinitz could, in fact,
bring political pressure to bear on the Nixon
administration. In fact, beginning on 7 October

the Israeli Ambassador had mentioned to Kissinger
the possibility of appealing to Israel's Congressional supporters. But Kissinger had asked
Dinitz not to "go public." Nixon by this time
was already in serious political trouble. The
Watergate Affair was deepening, and the Vice-
President was under judicial scrutiny for bribery
during his term as governor in Maryland. (On
10 October, Agnew resigned from the vice-presi-
dency after having pleaded no contest to charges
of tax evasion.) In the context of these problems,
Kissinger felt that Nixon could not afford a
breach of confidence in his foreign policy.

In the early hours of 13 October, Kissinger
was on the phone with Schlesinger, ordering him
to "get busy implementing the president's policy."
Next, he met with Nixon in the White House to
report on the Pentagon's obstructionist tactics.
According to the Kalbs:

> Nixon took immediate action. He
> instructed General Alexander Haig
> to order Schlesinger to send ten
> C-130 transport planes loaded with
> military supplies to the Azores at
> once; then to fly twenty C-130s
> directly to Israel; and finally to
> facilitate a quick Israeli pick up
> of the cargo left in the Azores.[57]

In order to eliminate any ambiguity, Nixon made
his orders more precise later that day during an
emergency meeting in the White House. After
listening to Schlesinger's explanations for the
delay, Nixon told the Secretary of Defense: "To
hell with the charters. Get the supplies there
with American military planes! Forget the Azores!
Get moving! I want no further delays."[58]

At 3:30 p.m. on Saturday, 13 October, Dinitz
received a phone call from the Pentagon. He was
informed that the first fleet of American C-130
transport planes had just left for Israel.[59]

21

This version of Kissinger's participation in
the decision to airlift military supplies to
Israel is interesting from a number of perspec-
tives. In the first instance, if correct, it
reveals the incapacity of the United States to
respond quickly in a crisis situation even when
the course of action has been decided on by the
two highest foreign policy decision-makers, the
President and the Secretary of State. The Israeli
ambassador first requested military assistance on
7 October, and was assured by 9 October that the
President had agreed to resupply Israeli losses.
Yet in spite of such apparent American willingness
to meet Israeli military needs, the first shipment
of supplies did not leave the United States for
Israel until 13 October, nearly a week after the
original request. The process is interesting
from another angle as well. The original plan
was for Israeli planes to land in the United States
to pick up supplies, but this was abandoned in
favor of chartering American airlines to deliver
the equipment. When this second option proved
unfeasible, it became necessary to use American
military transports to resupply Israel. The
sequence of events in this version of the airlift
decision strongly suggests that top officials
failed to seriously study the alternative methods
of shipment at the outset (as might be expected
in a rational decision-making process), and
instead more or less fished around for ad hoc
solutions until, in the end, it became necessary
to directly involve the United States military in
supplying the Israeli army. For example, at no
point was the feasibility of chartering American
airlines to deliver military supplies to Israel
seriously studied. Rather, this approach was
simply adopted on a trial and error basis, with
the consequent delay in the execution of a policy
decided on by the top echelon of the Nixon
Administration.

Two further observations which should be
made about this version of the airlift decision
are the influence of bureaucratic politics and
the role of political coercion that can exist

even in negotiations between parties working, on the surface at least, for the same objective. According to the above account, Secretary of Defense Schlesinger was the primary obstacle to getting the airlift under way even after 9 October when the President had reportedly agreed to resupply Israel. Yet, paradoxically, this does not prove that Schlesinger was directly disobeying presidential policy since Nixon had not definitively resolved the method of shipping supplies to Israel, which was a decision that therefore remained to be decided by the bureaucracy. Hence, although Schlesinger may have disagreed with the policy itself, he was able to use his position as a bureaucratic executive to delay the implementation of the policy without disobeying presidential policy by focusing on technical issues of implementation. Kissinger was unable to force Schlesinger to move more quickly, and in the end it required a direct order from Nixon himself to get the airlift under way. Turning to the second observation, it would appear that there was a good working relationship between Dinitz and Kissinger, and that both parties desired to expedite the shipment of military supplies to Israel. Nevertheless, it eventually became necessary for Dinitz to press Kissinger for immediate results by threatening to mobilize Israeli political supporters in the US Congress, which would have had severe repercussions for the Nixon White House. Whether this was the case or not, Kissinger did become more active in pressuring the Pentagon for action after Dinitz's threat. This demonstrates how necessary political leverage is even in supposedly cooperative endeavors.

The "anti-Kissinger" version blames the Secretary of State himself for the delay in the airlift to Israel. According to this view, Kissinger never had any intention of fulfilling Tel Aviv's military needs. His sympathetic promises to Dinitz were designed to stop the Israeli Ambassador from turning to Congress and the media for support.[60]

23

Why would Kissinger have reservations about sending supplies to Israel? After all, Israel was a close ally of the US, and, in the context of recent American foreign policy, the US should have provided Israel with military equipment when Tel Aviv needed such supplies. The explanation that is provided in the anti-Kissinger version for this seemingly contradictory behavior is twofold: dealing with one set of factors focusing on Kissinger's personal style; and a second set involving the broader issues of US policy during the war.

When the fighting broke out, Kissinger along with most other observers in Washington believed that the war would end quickly.[61] Some even thought that it could be ended within a few days-- that is, as soon as the Israeli reserves could be mobilized.[62] It was expected that Israel would score another major victory and that the result of the 1967 war would be repeated again. Given these assumptions, it has been suggested that:

> Kissinger calculated that the military aid to Israel, while not making the crucial difference in the field, could damage the still hoped-for cooperation with Moscow and future relations with the Arab countries.[63]

Kissinger was particularly concerned about American access to Middle Eastern oil. Throughout the summer, the oil-producing Arab countries had threatened to use an oil embargo against the United States if it provided military aid to Israel.[64] It was against this background, according to this second view, that the Secretary of State initially decided not to respond to Israel's requests for an airlift.

However, as early as 7 October, Israel's Ambassador was in Kissinger's office requesting military supplies. The Secretary knew that if

he flatly denied Dinitz's requests, Dinitz would
turn to Congress and the media for help. But,
as we have seen, Kissinger was determined to
avoid this since he felt that Nixon could not
afford a major clash with Congress. There was
strong support for Israel in Washington, and
little doubt that Congress would support Israel's
request.[65] The solution, it seemed, was to stop
Dinitz from "going public." This required
convincing the ambassador that Israel's needs
could be met through personal diplomacy and that
there was no necessity for a public outcry.
Thus, during the first few days of the fighting,
Kissinger developed a set of tactics to convince
Dinitz that he fully supported Israel and that the
ambassador could count on him to expedite military
assistance. Kissinger's accessibility to Dinitz
and the installation of a "hot line" to the
Israeli Embassy were both designed to gain his
trust.

According to this second version, the "bureaucratic obstructionism" that delayed the
airlift to Israel was orchestrated by Kissinger.
Even though Schlesinger might have had his own
reservations about an airlift to Israel based on
his concerns over an oil embargo, at no time did
he disobey orders or cause unnecessary delays.
The delaying tactics were all Kissinger's. It
was Kissinger who, for example, developed the
idea of hiring civilian charters--knowing that
the private airlines would not cooperate.
According to this version, Schlesinger:

> . . .favored in principle a resupply
> airlift flown by American military
> aircraft, but he was paralyzed by a
> White House policy directive, drafted
> by Kissinger, ordering a hold on
> such operations. The written direc-
> tive was a Kissingerian masterpiece
> of devious diplomacy. Its thrust
> was that the Pentagon would be
> represented to the Israelis by
> Kissinger as the "bad guys," refusing

to help, while the White House
and the State Department would
appear as the "good guys," fighting
a bureaucratic battle to aid Israel.[66]

By 9 October, reports from the battlefield
indicated that the war would last longer than
expected. While the Israelis were gaining the
upper hand on one front, they were involved in
a still uncertain struggle on the other front.
On the northern front, the Syrian forces were
beginning to falter. Not only had the Syrian
invasion been stopped, but it seemed that they
were beginning to retreat. But news from the
Sinai indicated a different outcome. The Bar-Lev
Line was destroyed, and Egyptian tanks were
moving toward the Mitla Pass. There was no
assurance of a quick Israeli victory.

Kissinger was among the first to realize
that the October War might result in a new
balance of power in the Middle East, particularly
if some of the variables were manipulated. The
Secretary of State believed, according to Edward
Sheehan, that "if he allowed neither side to win
decisively, then he might manipulate the results
to launch negotiations, and--ultimately--to
compose the Arab-Israeli quarrel."[67]   Thus,
according to this second version, the Secretary's
delaying tactics after 10 October were aimed at
stopping the Israelis from scoring another
decisive victory. Since the Arabs were performing
much better than had been expected, it was
believed that if Israel were to receive only
limited assistance, the fighting might result in
a military stalemate. Such an outcome would be
utilized by the Americans to force both sides
into political-military negotiations. "Having
suffered and lost, the Israelis could be
manipulated by remote control through the supply
of military equipment or its denial. They would
be forced to make territorial concessions."
Kissinger expected the Arabs, on their part,
would also become more flexible. "Having won
limited victory, the Egyptians would most probably

26

become more tractable, and Sadat would have established a political base which would allow him to make the required diplomatic concession."[68]

An authoritative assessment of American foreign policy during October 1973 requires access to many documents that remain classified at this time. Only after the personal papers of Kissinger and Schlesinger are made public can we fully know the reason(s) behind the delay in the American airlift to Israel. However, from the existing evidence we can draw some preliminary conclusions.

It seems that neither version of Kissinger's role in the issue provides a completely satisfying or logical explanation for the politics of the airlift to Israel. The pro-Kissinger version argues that the Secretary of State was willing to supply Israel with military hardware, but that the Defense Department refused to cooperate. The result of the Pentagon's posture was a considerable delay in the airlift to Israel. In light of the fact that prior to 10 October--in both versions--Kissinger expected a quick Israeli victory, it seems rather unlikely that the Secretary of State would rush to the aid of Israel. To the contrary, given the cost of close identification with the Tel Aviv government, it is quite plausible that Kissinger did indeed wish to delay supplying the Israelis.[69] During the Six-Day War, America's close association with Israel had resulted in Arab claims that Israel's quick victory was facilitated by direct American military assistance. There was no reason to give rise to such speculations again and, therefore, the anti-Kissinger version would appear in this respect to provide a more realistic description of the airlift politics.

Nevertheless, there are certain inconsistencies and problems with the anti-Kissinger explanation of the airlift decision, too. This second version argues that Kissinger's intention was to convince the Israeli ambassador that the

Nixon Administration was doing everything in its
power to resupply the Israeli army in order to
prevent Dinitz from taking his case to the
Congress and the American public. But because
Kissinger expected a swift Israeli victory he in
fact saw no need to endanger American relations
with the Arab world by directly involving the
United States in the October war on the side of
Israel. He therefore, according to this explanation of events, worked out a scenario in which
Secretary of Defense Schlesinger and the Pentagon
would play the role of obstructionists, while he
himself projected the image of doing everything
in his power to get the airlift of supplies
under way. In this fashion American entanglement
in the war could be put off (in the expectation
that the war would end before the US could be
involved) without a deterioration in American-
Israeli ties. The major flaw in this account of
events is the role supposedly played by Schlesinger. Given the lack of cooperation that
existed between the Secretary of State and the
Secretary of Defense, it is doubtful that
Schlesinger willingly allowed Kissinger to shift
all blame to the Defense Department and himself
for the delay in resupplying Israel, especially
since this could involve political costs for the
Secratary of Defense at some later point in time.
The suggestion of a conspiracy between the
Secretary of State and Secretary of Defense
contained in the second version of the airlift
decision therefore seems unrealistic.

If the anti-Kissinger account is at least
partially accurate, it seems likely that the
attempt to deceive the Israelis was Kissinger's
alone. Knowing that Schlesinger opposed supplying
Israel with American equipment, Kissinger may
have been able to enlist the unwitting help of
the Secretary of Defense without ever actually
letting the Defense Department know that he, too,
wanted to avoid antagonizing the Arabs by supplying
the Israelis. Thus, in the early stages he
allowed the Defense Department to hold up the
airlift. But after reports of the Soviet airlift

to the Arabs, Kissinger became convinced that an American response was required for reasons other than the military needs of the Israeli army. At that point, Kissinger's demands that the Secretary of Defense get the airlift underway became sincere. As events reveal, American military transports left for Israel within two days after Kissinger received reports of the extent of the Soviet resupply of Egypt and Syria, adding some credibility to this explanation of the airlift decision.

By the end of October, the United States had flown in some 22,395 tons of supplies in C-5 and C-141 freighters to Israel. This was supplemented by a further 5,500 tons carried by Israeli El Al aircrafts. The supplies included M-48 and M-60 tanks, CH-53 helicopters, F-4 Phantoms, A-4 Skyhawks, and anti-aircraft weapons.

The change from delaying tactics to a massive airlift to Israel, it would seem, can be best explained in terms of Soviet-American relations. As it was argued earlier, for Kissinger the Arab-Israeli conflict was basically a problem in Soviet-American relations. Prior to 10 October, the Soviet airlift to the Arabs was limited. By 11 October, Soviet aid to the Arabs became "massive." Not only were there reports that on the preceding day twenty-one Anatonov 22s had landed in Egypt and Syria, but there were also indications that "two large Soviet transport ships had steamed through the Bosporus heading toward the war zone."[11] For Kissinger, these developments were unacceptable. They could precipitate an apparent military imbalance between the superpowers. Thus, the Secretary decided that the United States would have to act. He had to demonstrate to the Soviets that Washington was unwilling to accept a political-military change in its position in the Middle East. Kissinger decided that the effect of the Soviet airlift to the Arabs had to be neutralized. This required a massive American airlift to Israel. Of course, what reinforced Kissinger's decision was that by this time domestic forces (the pro-Israeli lobby) were also beginning to pressure the administration. Therefore, international considerations, reinforced and probably legitimized by domestic politics, resulted in a dramatic shift in American policy. Not only were the Israeli demands for military aid met, but the equipment was shipped directly to Tel Aviv in American military planes.

From the foregoing discussion two general conclusions can be drawn. First, during 6-10 October, there was little serious concern in Washington that Israel might actually lose on the battlefield. Given its prior military record, decision-makers in Washington believed that Israel would be able to deal with the Arabs with only minimum outside assistance. There would be no need for American aid, particularly when any Washington involvement would damage America's position in the Arab world. Furthermore, any intentional delay in the shipment of arms to Israel would have to have had the tacit approval of both Kissinger and Schlesinger. The Secretary of Defense would not have played into Kissinger's delaying tactics if he had not agreed with them in principle.

The Cease-Fire

When the October War broke out, Washington's immediate reaction was to seek a meeting of the UN Security Council in order to establish the grounds for a cease-fire.[72] But the United States did not appeal for a cease-fire at the UN until 22 October. There were two primary reasons for this delay. First, Kissinger is thought to have had serious misgivings about the effectiveness of the Security Council. He believed that outcome of the war would be determined on the battlefield and not at the UN.[73] Second, and probably more important, was the lack of agreement between Moscow and Washington on the conditions for a cease-fire. During the early phase of the fighting, the Soviet Union seemed opposed to the idea of a cease-fire. To the extent that the USSR was willing to discuss a cease-fire, it was Moscow's position that the cease-fire should be linked to an Israeli withdrawal to pre-1967 borders. This condition, of course, was rejected by both Kissinger and Israeli Prime Minister Golda Meir,[74] both of whom expected a quick Israeli victory.

On 10 October, there was a change in the Soviet position. Moscow dropped its demand for a return to the 1967 borders. By that date, Moscow was ready to call for a cease-fire "in place." One reason for this change was that, "the Soviet Union had reached the conclusion that the goals they had set for themselves had been in large measure achieved."[75] The Arabs had obtained a limited victory, had recaptured some of their lost lands and, most importantly, they had regained their confidence. Another consideration behind this change in the Soviet position was Moscow's assessment of Arab capabilities. Even though the Arabs had performed well in battle, "the Soviets feared . . . that the longer the war went on, the more likely it became that the Egyptians would suffer major military reverses, which would lead in turn to incalculable prospects of escalation."[76] The change to a cease-fire "in place" reflected Soviet pessimism about the long-term military capabilites of the Arabs.

America's reaction to the Soviet's call for cease-fire "in place" was negative. After consulting with the Israelis, Kissinger informed Dobrynin that the "United States would agree to co-sponsor a cease-fire initiative that would provide for a return to the pre-war lines."[77] A cease-fire "in place," Kissinger believed, would be "a death blow to any attempt to achieve an acceptable political agreement after the war."[78]

According to Matti Golan, on 12 October--two days after Israel and the United States rejected the Soviet call for a cease-fire "in place"--Mrs. Meir decided that the Soviet proposal was not totally unacceptable after all. The Israelis had suffered a devastating blow, at least in the Sinai. The Prime Minister was now somewhat doubtful about Israeli military capabilities. Besides, the Israelis were running out of supplies, and there was still no sign of an American airlift. Thus, once the Soviet Union reintroduced its offer of the cease-fire "in place," she decided to accept i According to Golan, after Kissinger was informed o Meir's decision he began working out the details and the question of who would offer the cease-fire resolution.[79] However, while the tactical questio were being worked out, the situation in the battle field changed dramatically. On 14 October Israeli forces crossed the Suez Canal and the Egyptian advance in the Sinai was stopped. Everything indi cated that the direction of the battle was changin in favor of the Israelis. Thus, by 16 October, Mr Meir withdrew her earlier acceptance of a cease- fire "in place." Now, the Israelis again insiste that they would accept a cease-fire only if the Arab forces were withdrawn to the pre-October 197 borders. The Soviet Union thereafter became the party most concerned with achieving an immediate cease-fire.

Moscow Pushes for a Cease-Fire

Soviet motives and behavior during the Octob War have been subjected to a number of conflictin interpretations. Some have argued that Soviet behavior was consistent with the principle of detente between the US and the USSR. Others have suggested that Soviet policy during October was accordance with traditional Soviet foreign policy viz., that Soviet behavior was aimed at maximizir local gains.[80] Whichever interpretations one may adopt, however, one point remains clear. In

October 1973, the Soviet Union was not prepared to accept an Arab defeat. Another Israeli victory would have damaged Soviet prestige not only in the Middle East but world-wide. Moreover, another defeat would have weakened the position of pro-Soviet leaders in the region.

Thus, as the direction of the battle changed, anxiety grew in Moscow. What particularly disturbed the Soviets was the news of the Israeli Suez-crossing and the fact that the Egyptians themselves showed little concern for the Israeli presence on the west bank of the canal.[81] Moscow learned about the crossing late on 15 October. The next day, Soviet Premier Kosygin flew secretly to Cairo to convince Sadat that it was time for a cease-fire.

Kosygin's trip to Cairo lasted three days. Initially, the Egyptians demanded that any cease-fire proposal be linked to UN Resolution 242.[82]

But by October 18, while still in Cairo, Kosygin had received detailed information on the magnitude of the Israeli presence on the west bank. The Israeli presence represented more than just a symbolic force as the Egyptians had previously thought.[83] Kosygin impressed this point on Sadat and, after intensive bargaining with him, the Egyptians accepted a Soviet proposal calling for a cease-fire "in place." According to Sadat, the proposal to which he gave his consent called for: 1) a cease-fire guaranteed by the superpowers; 2) an American-Soviet guarantee of a total Israeli withdrawal; and 3) the convening of a peace conference, under United Nations auspices, to achieve a total settlement.[84] According to Egyptian sources, Sadat was assured by Kosygin that the Soviets were prepared to guarantee the cease-fire by themselves if the Americans failed to do so.[85] It was in the context of these assurances that Sadat gave his approval to the Soviet cease-fire proposal.

Kosygin returned to Moscow on 19 October.

The next day Kissinger received an invitation from
Brezhnev to fly to Moscow for "urgent consultations
on the Middle East."[86]   Kissinger was told that if
he could not accept the Soviet invitation, Moscow
was prepared to send Gromyko to the United States.

For a variety of reasons, Kissinger decided
to accept the invitation. First, the trip to
Moscow would give him the opportunity to take
personal charge of the negotiation. Second, and
more important, was the element of time. Kissinger
thought that he could control the pace of the
negotiations--to the advantage of the Israelis--
with the Soviets.[87]   Both Kissinger and the Israeli
by this point in the war realized that time was on
the side of Tel Aviv. The longer the battle
continued, the better the Israeli military position
and, ultimately, the Israeli bargaining position
became. Kissinger assured Dinitz prior to his
departure for Moscow that he "would do all he could
do to slow down the talks." According to Matti
Golan, Kissinger even told Dinitz that "upon his
arrival at Vanukov Airport near Moscow, he would
tell his Soviet hosts that he was tired from the
trip and wished to begin the discussion only on
the following day.[88]

Whether Matti Golan's account is accurate or
not, Kissinger behaved quite differently. Once
in Moscow, the Secretary wasted no time in meeting
with Brezhnev. Only two hours after his arrival
in Moscow, Kissinger was in Brezhnev's Kremlin
office discussing the details of a cease-fire.[89]

Nixon granted complete authority to Kissinger
to negotiate with the Soviets in the name of the
United States during this trip.[90]   Although this
reflected Nixon's confidence in his Secretary of
State, it was also indicative of the President's
preoccupation with his own domestic problems. On
20 October, Nixon dismissed Archibald Cox, the
first Watergate Special Prosecutor, which led to
the departure of the two top officials in the
Department of Justice--Elliot Richardson and
William Ruckelshaus. This series of events

34

(known as the "Saturday Night Massacre"), together with the earlier forced resignation of Vice President Agnew, had created so much political controversy that Nixon felt obliged to concentrate fully on his domestic problems, leaving foreign affairs to Kissinger.[91]

Kissinger's trip to Moscow lasted about forty hours, during which time Kissinger and Brezhnev worked out the details of the cease-fire. By 21 October, both the US and the USSR had agreed on the terms for the termination of hostilities. The Soviet Union favored a cease-fire because Moscow was convinced that the Arab position would continue to deteriorate as long as the fighting continued. The Israeli troops on the west bank of the Suez were beginning to outflank the Egyptian forces, and on the Syrian front the Israelis were only twenty miles away from Damascus. Besides the situation on the battlefield, Brezhnev was also concerned about the possible consequences of the war for US-USSR relations. On the third day of fighting, the Soviet leader had received a letter from President Nixon reminding the Russians of their obligations outlined in two joint communiques signed by the US and the USSR in May 1972 and June 1973. Under the terms of these communiques, the two sides agreed to "act in such a manner as to prevent the development of situations capable of causing a dangerous exacerbation of their relations, as to avoid military confrontations, and as to exclude the outbreak of nuclear war between them and between either of the Parties and other countries."[92] The situation in the Middle East after 16 October had begun to bring the two superpowers closer to such a confrontation. Aware of this, Brezhnev became more eager to observe the spirit of these two joint communiques.

Kissinger also favored a cease-fire, but his reasons were more complicated. If the war lasted a few more days, the Israelis would completely defeat the Arabs. This would strengthen the Israeli bargaining position and remove the possibility of a compromise that would establish a basis for long-term peace in the area. But if the war ended in a stalemate, Kissinger could play a personal role in bringing about a negotiated settlement.

Furthermore, Kissinger was concerned about the threat of an oil cutoff. While aboard his plane to Moscow, Kissinger received word that the government of Saudi Arabia had announced a ten percent reduction in oil production and an embargo[93] of oil shipments to the United States. The Saudi's decision had followed an earlier announcement by the Arab oil ministers that oil production would be cut by five percent each month until[94] Israel had withdrawn from all Arab territories. Although the US itself was not affected drastically by the decision of the Arab oil-producing countries (Arab oil then accounted for only twelve percent of US consumption), the reduction could have been disastrous for Western Europe and Japan[95] which were almost totally dependent on Arab oil. Thus, Kissinger, like Brezhnev, had his own particular reasons for calling for a cease-fire.

Nevertheless, there was some disagreement on what form the cease-fire accord should take. Brezhnev argued that the cease-fire should be unconditional. Kissinger, on the other hand, believed that the cease-fire should be linked to peace talks. In Kissinger's view, a cease-fire "in place" which was not conditional upon some sort of future negotiation between the combatants would freeze the situation, and another war would soon break out. Kissinger thus insisted on linking the cease-fire to peace talks between Egypt and Israel. Initially, Brezhnev seemed reluctant to accept the position since Sadat had opposed any such idea. This obstacle was overcome, however, by a Soviet promise to the Egyptian president that if he agreed to a cease-fire proposal linked to direct talks between the Egyptians and the Israelis, the USSR "would--if necessary, alone-- guarantee the observance of the cease-fire."[96] On Sunday, 21 October, Brezhnev and Kissinger were able to agree on the text of a cease-fire

resolution that was introduced in the Security
Council the next day. The cease-fire, which was
adopted unanimously, called upon all parties to
cease fighting within twelve hours after the
adoption of the resolution. The resolution also
instructed the parties to begin implementing
Security Council Resolution 242. In addition, the
two sides were called upon to begin negotiations
"under appropriate auspices aimed at establishing
a just and durable peace in the Middle East."[97]

The cease-fire went into effect at 6:52 p.m.
(Middle East time) on 22 October, but the fighting
continued in some areas, and there were charges and
countercharges of cease-fire violations. Although
it is not yet known which party violated the cease-
fire first,[98] it was the Israeli cease-fire violations on the west bank of the canal that were
the most flagrant and, therefore, dangerous. By
their initiatives, the Israeli forces encircled
the Egyptian Third Army on the west bank and
thereby cut the over land supply line to the
20,000 Egyptian forces on both sides of the canal.[99]

The encirclement of the Egyptian Third Army
did not in itself change the outcome of the war,
since the Arabs had lost the initiative as early as
16 October. What it did do was significantly
enhance the Israeli negotiating position, effectively
cancelling out many of the psychological and
political accomplishments which Egypt achieved
early in the conflict. Moreover, the encirclement
of the 20,000 Egyptian forces in the Sinai represented a personal defeat for President Sadat.
As a result, there was even speculation that his
regime might be overthrown.[100] However, the single
most important consideration in the Israeli
cease-fire violation that encircled the Egyptian
Third Army was the impunity with which it was
carried out. Sadat realized that having met no
effective international resistence to their cease-
fire violation, the Israelis would be encouraged
to continue to disregard the cease-fire, and
Egypt was no longer in a military position to
defend itself. For these reasons, therefore,

Sadat turned immediately to the Soviet Union
for assistance in enforcing the cease-fire.

The Soviets reacted quickly upon learning of
the Israeli cease-fire violation. In a strong
statement, the Soviet Union warned Israel of grave
consequences for such violations. According to
an official statement in Izvestia on 25 October:

> The Soviet government and the entire
> Soviet people angrily protest these
> perfidious actions by the Israeli
> government and demand that Israel
> immediately cease fire, stop all
> military operations against troops
> of the Arab states, and withdraw
> its troops to the October 22 cease-
> fire line, in accordance with the
> Security Council decision of
> October 22, 1973.
>
> The Soviet government warns the Israeli
> government that the continuation of
> its aggressive actions against the
> Arab Republic of Egypt and the Syrian
> Arab Republic will entail very
> serious consequences.[101]

The Soviets had extracted agreement to the cease-
fire from Sadat on the condition that the two
superpowers would enforce its provisions. Brezhnev
had received Kissinger's assurance of US cooperation
on this point.[102] The Soviets believed Israel would
not undertake such actions without at least a
tacit US approval. Thus, from the Soviet per-
spective, the cease-fire amounted to a "carefully
prepared criminal and hypocritical imperialist
provocation."[103] Moscow gradually became convinced
that the Israeli move had Kissinger's personal
blessing.[104]

There are conflicting reports concerning
Kissinger's role in the Israeli cease-fire violations. According to the Kalbs, Kissinger's
sympathetic biographers, the Secretary of State

was not aware of the Israeli cease-fire violations until after they occurred. Indeed, according to the Kalbs, he became "furious" when he heard the news.[105] A similar view is expressed by the Insight team of the London Sunday Times. According to this version, upon hearing the news of the Israeli cease-fire violation, Kissinger told an aide: "My God, the Russians will think I double-crossed them." After pausing a moment he continued, "And in their shoes, who wouldn't?"[106]

However, Matti Golan, whose The Secret Conversations of Henry Kissinger: Step-by-Step Diplomacy in the Middle East was banned in Israel, argues that the Israeli cease-fire violations had the tacit approval of Kissinger. He states that when Kissinger stopped in Israel on his way back from Moscow on 23 October, he implied to Israeli officials that the cease-fire did not have to go into effect immediately. According to Golan, during his meeting with Israeli officials Kissinger came under severe criticism for not allowing them to "finish the job." Thus, Golan reports:

> Stung by the criticism, Kissinger finally asked how many days the army needed to complete the encirclement of the two Egyptian armies on the east bank of the Suez Canal. Chief of Staff Elazar put it at around seven days, but the Air Force Chief, Brigadier General Peled, excitedly argued that now, without their air defense umbrella of SAM missiles, it was possible to destroy the two armies in two or three days. Kissinger responded: "Two or three days? That's all? Well, in Vietnam the cease-fire didn't go into effect at the exact time that was agreed on.[107]

It is impossible at this time to establish with any degree of certainty Kissinger's role in Israel's cease-fire violations. It is conceivable the Secretary may have alluded to the cease-fire

violations that occured in Vietnam. But the crucial
question is what was implied in the statement. Was
Kissinger giving his advance approval to Israeli
cease-fire violations? If that were the case, how
does one account for Kissinger's reported reaction
after the cease-fire? In addition to private
remarks to his aides and newsmen, there is other
evidence that suggests Kissinger disapproved of
Israel's actions. On 23 October, the US and the
USSR co-sponsored a new resolution in the Security
Council which called for "immediate cessation of
all kinds of firing and of all military actions
and urges that the forces be returned to the
positions they occupied at the moment the cease-
fire became effective." Of course the possibility
exists that the US action in the UN was simply a
diplomatic gesture and that the US did not expect
the Israelis to abide by the terms of this resolution. But Kissinger seemed equally alarmed even
in private. According to Dayan, once Kissinger
learned about the encirclement of the Egyptian
army he called Mrs. Meir and threatened that,
"Should Israel not observe the cease-fire, the
United States would not stand in the way of Soviet
actions to enforce it."[108]

In the light of Kissinger's reported reactions
both public and private, it would therefore seem
reasonable to conclude that the cease-fire violations were planned and executed by Israel without
Washington's prior knowledge or approval. Kissinger did not play a role in the encirclement of the
Third Army. In fact, the advantage that the
Israelis gained by encircling the Egyptian Third
Army actually worked against Kissinger's efforts
to end the war in a stalemate. Only if both
sides failed to achieve a military victory did
Kissinger believe he would be in a position to
force the parties into comprehensive talks over
the issues affecting peace in the region.

One possibility that should be considered is
that Kissinger understood that any cease-fire
agreement could not be imposed in the Middle East
without the acceptance of the Israeli cabinet,

40

and that the cabinet would be unlikely to agree
to a proposal that would stop the Israeli army
just short of a major military victory. The Secretary of State may therefore have felt it necessary to be purposely vague on the subject of the
effective date of the cease-fire accord in order
to secure Israeli acceptance. Once Israel had
officially agreed to the cease-fire, the United
States would then be able to pressure the Israelis
to abide by its terms, however displeased the Tel
Aviv government might be. In other words, Kissinger may have intentionally permitted the Israelis
to believe that Washington would not oppose
cease-fire violations without, in fact, ever
explicitly saying so. Otherwise, Kissinger may
have considered Israeli acceptance of the cease-
fire impossible to obtain. Therefore, if the
Secretary of State was actually "surprised" by
Israel's violations of the accord, it was a surprise for which he himself had laid the ground
work. In point of fact, it was probably the
Israelis who were most surprised by Kissinger's
reaction since at that point they must have realized that they had been maneuvered into a cease-
fire agreement that the American Secretary of
State had actually intended to enforce from the
outset.

The Alert

Sadat reacted to Israel's cease-fire violation by appealing to the superpowers. In a private message to Nixon and Brezhnev on 24 October,
he called upon the United States and the Soviet
Union to send their troops to the Middle East
for the purpose of insuring the cease-fire.[109]
Sadat also repeated his request in the Security
Council. On 24 October, the Egyptian Foreign
Minister urged the council "to call on the Soviet
Union and the United States each . . . to send
forces immediately from the forces stationed near
the area to supervise the implementation of the
cease-fire. . . ."[110]

The Soviet Union reacted favorably to Sadat's
request. On the evening of 24 October, Soviet
Ambassador Dobrynin informed Kissinger that the
Soviet representative in the Security Council had
instructions to support a proposal by the non-
aligned nations for a big-power police force.
According to the Kalbs, Kissinger "suspected that
the Russians were actively encouraging such a
proposal, and, in fairly blunt language, he
urged Dobrynin to tell Moscow that the United
States vigorously opposed the idea."[111] The
Secretary of State opposed the introduction of
American troops into the Middle East for a number
of reasons.[112] In the first instance, he feared
that troops originally deployed to police a cease-
fire would, in time, become the object of Arab
terrorist attacks. Then, the stage would be set
for an escalation of the American military presence
first in order to guarantee the security of
American cease-fire observers and, later, to
combat Arab terrorism. The danger of backing
into a protracted conflict in the region seemed
to far outweigh any possible advantages of sending
American forces into the Middle East. Secondly,
the presence of American military personnel in
the region would focus Arab grievances on the
United States which in turn could only harm
Washington's relations in the Arab world, providing
a wider range of issues of possible tension and
conflict. Lastly, the presence of American troops
might legitimize a Soviet military presence in
the region. And once Soviet troops had been
deployed, the United States would have virtually
no effective means of forcing their removal at
some future point. Hence, a joint US-Soviet peace
keeping force would pose the problem of bilateral
agreement on when to pull the force out of the
area, and the United States would be obliged to
keep troops in the Middle East until the Soviets
determined to withdraw theirs, or withdraw American troops unilaterally, leaving the Soviet Union
as the dominant military force in the region.
Neither of these were viewed as acceptable alter-
natives by Kissinger. Hence, the Secretary of
State viewed a joint US-Soviet military force as

a time bomb that could easily lead to a superpower conflict.[113]

The sequence of events that followed are still not completely agreed on. According to the Kalbs, the next move came at 9:25 p.m., when Dobrynin called Kissinger on the phone and read him the contents of a "very urgent" letter from Brezhnev. A secretary, listening in on an extension, took the four-paragraph text in shorthand. Ten minutes later, Kissinger read the transcript to Dobrynin to check it for accuracy. The text was confirmed by the Soviet ambassador.

According to the Kalbs, Brezhnev's letter "began with an unusually cool saluation." It began with "Mr. President," instead of the usual "My Dear Mr. President." The first paragraph began with a Soviet criticism of Israel for "brazenly challenging both the Soviet Union and the United States." Next, the Soviet leader stated that:

> Let us together. . . urgently dispatch Soviet and American con-tingents to Egypt. . .(The cease-fire had to be observed) without delay. . .I will say it straight that if you find it impossible to act together with us in this manner, we should be faced with the necessity urgently to consi-der the question of taking appro-priate steps unilaterally. Israel cannot be allowed to get away with the violations.[114]

According to the Kalbs' version--the most detailed account on the text of the letter--there is no evidence that the Soviet leader made any specific warning against Tel Aviv. However, according to some analysts, the letter also contained a direct threat to destroy the State of Israel.[115]

Upon receipt of Brezhnev's letter, Kissinger

called Nixon and advised him that "the United
States might have to alert its military forces
as one way of deterring any unilateral Soviet
move."[116] The President agreed and authorized
the Secretary to make the necessary preparations.
Kissinger, in turn, met with three members of the
National Security Council (NSC): James Schlesinger,
William Colby (Director of the CIA), and Admiral
Thomas Moore (Chairman of the Joint Chiefs of
Staff), the last two participated in the meeting
only in an advisory capacity. Referring to
Kissinger's dual role as the Secretary of State
and advisor to the president on national security
affairs, an aide later described the NSC participants as Kissinger, Kissinger, and Schlesinger.
This small group met in the White House at 11 p.m.
to decide on the proper response to the Brezhnev
letter.[117]

Throughout the NSC deliberations on the
evening of 24 October, President Nixon remained
on the second floor of the White House, and did
not participate in the meeting. Indeed, during
the entire period of the fourth Arab-Israeli War,
Nixon remained in the background. It was Kissinger who met daily with Dinitz and Dobrynin, and
it was the Secretary who was responsible for
engineering the air-lift, the cease-fire, and the
alert. During this crucial period, Nixon was
preoccupied with the Watergate Affair which had
virtually paralyzed his presidency. Thus, as a
matter of necessity, not choice, Nixon left the
Middle East to Kissinger--not only during October,
but also in the months that followed.

The NSC meeting of 24 October lasted for about
an hour. At 12.05 a.m., the participants decided
to accept Kissinger's recommendations. American
forces were put on a world-wide nuclear alert--
Defense Condition Three.[118] At 1:30 a.m., the
aircraft carrier, John F. Kennedy, was ordered
from the Eastern Atlantic into the Mediterranean,
and the 82nd Airborne Division at Fort Bragg,
North Carolina, was ordered to be ready to move
by 6:00 a.m.

The military alert is one of the most puzzling and controversial aspects of the Kissinger-Nixon foreign policy during the war. During the crisis, Kissinger promised that shortly after the war he would provide more detailed information on the sequence of events leading to the alert.[119] But no additional information was ever released by the Secretary of State. After seven years, the following questions still remain unresolved:

1) Did Kissinger actually receive a threatening letter from Brezhnev the evening of 24 October?

2) Did the available intelligence data support the credibility of a Soviet threat of intervention?

3) Was the sole objective of the American alert to deter the Soviet Union from intervening in the Middle East, or was it also aimed at the Israelis to scare them into observing the cease-fire?

4) Was the alert motivated, in part at least, by Watergate?

The alert was supposedly triggered by the Brezhnev letter--a letter which, according to Kissinger, was threatening and brutal. It is this letter which can best help determine the soundness of Kissinger's behavior. However, the letter has still not been made public, and some observers have even expressed doubts about its very existence.[120] Indeed, there is some mystery about the letter. According to the Kalbs, the Brezhnev letter was read to Kissinger over the telephone at 9:25 p.m. According to the insight team of the London Sunday Times, which has written one of the most comprehensive accounts of the war, the letter was delivered to Kissinger by Dobrynin at 10:45 p.m.[121] This apparent discrepency can be resolved by noting that it is not unusual for important diplomatic messages to be delivered verbally for the sake of time, with written copies

provided shortly after for the sake of accuracy and
diplomatic protocol.

Although the existence and substance of the
letter can be established only after it has been
made public, there is evidence that suggests
Kissinger did in fact receive an urgent note from
the Soviet leader. To begin with, there were
various communications exchanged between Moscow
and Washington during the crisis. There is nothing
to exclude the possibility of a letter from
Brezhnev on 24 October. Indeed, the seriousness
of the Israeli violations makes the existence of
some sort of protest from Moscow not only possible,
but quite probable.

The letter has been referred to by many
analysts. However, almost all the published works
are based either on Kissinger's own statements or
the Kalbs' account.[122] There is, however, one
independent source whose reference to the letter
is not based on either version. Ray S. Cline, the
director of the Bureau of Intelligence and
Research (INR) of the State Department, and a
critic of Dr. Kissinger, also refers to the
Brezhnev letter in an article written for Foreign
Policy. According to Cline, "At 9:25 p.m., Soviet
Ambassador Dobrynin delivered a strong message to
Kissinger from Brezhnev urging joint US-Soviet
action to enforce the cease-fire and ending with
a crucial sentence applying diplomatic pressure."[123]
Cline thus corroborates the Kalbs' account.

Once the news of the alert became public, the
United States came under severe criticism from the
Soviets. The Soviet Union accused the United
States of "over-reacting," and claimed that their
own actions were aimed "strictly at facilitating
the fulfillment of the Security Council's decisions on a cease-fire and the restoration of peace
in the Near East."[124] It is important to note
that the Soviet Union did not deny the existence
of the "Brezhnev letter." What Moscow claimed
was that Washington had misinterpreted Soviet
intentions. It seems logical that to the extent

that the American alert had been justified in
terms of the existence of a "brutal" message from
Moscow, the Soviets would have made a disclaimer
if Brezhnev had not sent such a message to
Kissinger on 24 October.

Even though there is some discrepancy
between the Kalb's account and the Insight Team
as to how the message was delivered to Kissinger,
there is a great deal of similarity between the
two accounts of the letter. According to the
Insight Team, the letter contained the following
important passage:

> We strongly urge that we both send
> forces to enforce the cease-fire, and
> if you do not, we may be obliged to
> consider acting alone.[125]

According to Marvin and Bernard Kalb, the letter
read in part:

> Let us together . . . urgently dis-
> patch Soviet and American contingents
> to Egypt . . . (the cease-fire had to
> be observed) without delay . . . if
> you find it impossible to act together
> with us in this manner, we should be
> faced with the necessity . . . of
> taking appropriate steps unilaterally.[126]

Although circumstantial evidence supports
the existence of the Brezhnev Letter, the crucial
question is whether the message justified the
nuclear alert. According to Kissinger, the alert
was called because "we became aware of the
alerting of certain Soviet representations in the
discussion that took place in the message from
Brezhnev"[127] The Secretary of State's remarks
were deliberately vague. But the Secretary of
Defense went into more detail on what Kissinger
referred to as "the alerting of certain Soviet
units." In his press conference on 26 October,
Schlesinger said:

We were aware that the Soviets had
alerted comprehensively their airborne
forces. In addition, the Soviet air
was stood down, I believe, starting
on Monday (22 October) and diminished
to zero flights on Tuesday. (Suggesting
that equipment was being mobilized
for Soviet intervention.)[128]

From the statement by Kissinger and Schlesinger,
it can be surmised that the alert was triggered
by two developments: 1) the threat of intervention reportedly contained in the Brezhnev letter,
and 2) intelligence reports indicating Soviet
military preparations. In an effort to analyze
the soundness of the alert, we will examine both
of these factors.

Kissinger has claimed that the Brezhnev
Letter posed an immediate threat to US interests
and, according to some reports, may even have
contained a specific threat against the State of
Israel.[129] From what is available, however,
these charges cannot be definitively confirmed.
The most detailed report of the letter is the
excerpt in Kissinger, by the Secretary of State's
sympathetic biographers, Marvin and Bernard Kalb.
But even in their version, there is no reference
to a Soviet threat against Israel. Probably the
most crucial, and what might be considered
threatening, statement that has been reported
was the part of the letter in which Brezhnev
allegedly warned: "I will say it straight, that
if you find it impossible to act together with us
in this matter, we should be faced with the
necessity urgently to consider the question of
taking appropriate steps unilaterally." The
passage, if accurately reported, clearly contained
an explicit threat of unilateral Soviet intervention in support of the Egyptians if the US
refused to cooperate in enforcing the cease-fire.
But equally important, the diplomatic note--so far
as we have been told--did not specifically
commit the Soviet Union to a direct military

intervention, nor did it close the door to counter proposals by the US for none-military enforcement of the cease-fire. What we do know for certain is that in an extremely brief period of time a mere handful of top officials (at most three) decided that the only appropriate response to the Brezhnev Letter was a nuclear alert.

Thus, the decision to place American nuclear forces on alert contained all of the characteristics of a "crisis decision." Specifically, options were apparently perceived as extremely narrow, the stakes were considered high, the time frame of the decision-making process short, the available concrete data scant, and the number of participants very small. The point is not that the Soviet message posed no threat to US interests, or did not demand an immediate and forceful US response. Rather, what we are suggesting is that there may have been alternative responses short of a nuclear alert which were never even considered. In fact, there is no indication that any effort was made by Washington to engage Moscow in a dialogue on a non-military, bilateral solution to the cease-fire question which might have gained valuable time for compromise or reflection on the consequences of competing courses of action. Moreover, it is important to stress that Kissinger's response was directed against the Soviet Union, and not against Israel whose cease-fire violations precipitated the crisis.

In short, the Brezhnev Letter may indeed have been provocative, but it does not appear to have been an ultimatum. From what we know of events, it seems plausible that a US response rejecting any superpower military intervention, but promising to bring immediate and effective pressure on Israel to observe the cease-fire, could have achieved the same effect as the nuclear alert at less risk. If one were to argue in response to this that the US could not have guaranteed Israeli compliance with the cease-fire, then one would be forced to admit that Kissinger was not, as he is so often described, a realist. One of the cardinal rules

49

of realism as outlined by Hans Morganthau, after
all, is that a nation should never allow a weaker
ally to dictate policy.

Our argument that the nuclear alert may have
been an unnecessary example of "brinksmanship" is
supported by the fact that it is far from certain
that the Soviet Union planned a large scale military operation in the Middle East. According to
Tad Szulc:

> . . . top intelligence officials
> say there was nothing to indicate
> that the Soviets were preparing
> an invasion. If anything, they
> said the Russians may have been
> pulling together a force requested
> by Sadat to join with the Americans
> in a peace-keeping operation.[130]

Some have even argued that the intelligence reports
did not support the theory of even a limited
Soviet intervention. According to a memo written
shortly after the alert, Cline informed Kissinger
that:

> In view of some of the unwarranted
> criticism of the government for
> its decision, I regret that you
> never advised your State Depart-
> ment intelligence arm that you
> had a problem nor asked us for
> an opinion on the evidence of
> Soviet intention to intervene
> with troops in the Mideast.
> Certainly the technical intelli-
> gence evidence available in INR
> did not support such a Soviet
> intention.[131]

To be sure, on 24 October some seven Soviet
airborne divisions were placed on alert.[132] But
"this alert had been in effect throughout the
war and had been known by Washington for at least
five or six days."[133] Thus, it seems unlikely

50

that this alone was the cause of the American
alert.

In his press conference of 26 October, the
Secretary of Defense stated that the American
alert had been necessitated by both military and
diplomatic indicators. After referring to the
Soviet alert, Schlesinger told reporters that:
"in addition, there were a number of other indicators of a military intelligence nature into
which I shan't go."[134]   It has been speculated
that Schlesinger was referring to CIA reports
indicating that the Soviets furnished the
Egyptians with nuclear warheads.[135]   Hence, the
alert, some have argued, was a signal to the
Soviets and to the Egyptians that the United
States would not tolerate the destruction of
Israel.

However, no concrete evidence was ever produced to show that either Egypt possessed nuclear
weapons or that the Soviets were planning to
transfer nuclear warheads to the Arabs. After
examining the relevant evidence, Senators Syming-
ton and Stennis of the Armed Services Committee
stated that there were no nuclear weapons in
Egypt during October.[136]   Even Kissinger himself
admitted this. In his press conference of
21 November he was asked whether the "Soviet
Union has introduced tactical nuclear weapons
into Egypt." The Secretary responded by saying
that:

> We have no confirmed evidence that
> the Soviet Union has introduced
> nuclear weapons into Egypt. And
> there are Soviet public statements
> rejecting this allegation. If the
> Soviet Union were to introduce
> nuclear weapons into local conflict,
> this would be a very grave matter
> and would be a fundamental shift
> in traditional practices . . . .[137]

In the traditional Soviet behavior there is

51

nothing that would point to a willingness to
furnish nuclear weapons to its clients.

There have been other reports suggesting
that the Egyptians possessed nuclear weapons as
in intelligence data reporting the passage of
nuclear material through the Bosporus. But even
if the report had been interpreted as serious in
Washington, it still could not have triggered
the alert. The report that a Soviet ship carrying
"nuclear material" had passed through the Bosporus
did not reach Washington until 25 October--when
the alert was already in full swing.[138]

President Nixon, referring to the alert in
a press conference on 26 October, stated that:

> It was a real crisis. It was the
> most difficult crisis we have had
> since the Cuban confrontation of
> 1962. But because we had had an
> initiative with the Soviet Union,
> because I had a basis of communi-
> cation with Mr. Brezhnev, we not
> only avoided a confrontation, but
> we moved a great step forward to-
> ward real peace in the Middle
> East.[139]

Within the context of the information we have
reviewed, Nixon's evaluation of the situation
appears to have been somewhat exaggerated. What
hard data is available about events leading up to
the alert does not incontravertably establish the
fact that there was a serious threat of a large
Soviet intervention into the Middle East.[140] This
is not to suggest that there was no possibility
whatever of a limited Soviet intervention, or
to imply that a limited Soviet intervention would
not have harmed US interests in the region.
Rather, the point is that the threat of Soviet
intervention during the October War was in no way
comparable to the Cuban missile crisis, and in
terms of the potential for escalation, there was
certainly less tension between the US and USSR in

52

1973 than in 1970 (during the civil war in Jordan).
Kissinger's statement on 25 October appears to
have been a far more accurate assessment of the
situation than the President's. Stated Kissinger:
"We do not now consider ourselves to be in a
confrontation with the Soviet Union . . . We are
not talking of a missile crisis-type situation."[141]
Therefore, the nuclear alert during the October
War cannot be explained in terms of the variables
that produced the alert during the confrontation
over Cuba.

If the US did not consider itself in a military confrontation with the Soviet Union, what
then justified the nuclear alert? There are
three possible explanations. First, one could
argue that Kissinger's decision was based on an
irrational consideration: that the Secretary of
State simply panicked when he read the Brezhnev
letter and decided to put the American forces on
alert. While this explanation might have served
for such persons as Rogers or Sisco, it seems
unlikely that it could be applied to Kissinger.
Beginning in 1969, Kissinger had been involved in
delicate negotiation with the Vietnamese, Chinese,
and the Russians. He had gone through a similarly
dangerous experience during the civil war in
Jordan. Of all the people who might have panicked,
Kissinger would seem the least likely candidate.

Another explanation wich some analysts
have offered is that the American military alert
was aimed at Tel Aviv and not just Moscow.[142]
Kissinger did not want the Israelis to continue
their cease-fire violations since that would have
made an overall peace settlement more difficult.
According to Sheehan: "Kissinger had no intention
to allow the Israelis to conclude the war with a
smashing conquest. That would have disgraced the
Egyptians, as in 1967, and demolished the prospect
of productive negotiations."[143] Furthermore, the
Secretary of State believed that "a clear-cut
Israeli victory would contribute to a further isolation of Israel, and, given American close ties
to the Jewish state, encourage a new wave of

53

anti-Americanism in the Middle East."[144]   The
Israelis had to be contained, and this required
that the Israelis be convinced that their cease-
fire violations would not be tolerated by Moscow
and that the Soviet Union was ready to militarily
intervene if the Israelis did not observe the
cease-fire. To convince Israel of the absolute
necessity of observing the cease-fire, Kissinger
needed to make the threat of Soviet intervention
appear credible. This required that Washington
put its forces on alert. According to Tad Szulc,
"Kissinger involved the threat of a Soviet intervention to force Israel to desist from destroying
a trapped Egyptian army."[145]

There may be some validity to this theory.
After Kissinger's trip to Moscow (19 October), the
Secretary's efforts, according to one source,
"were directed chiefly at stopping the Israeli
offensive and rescuing the encircled Egyptians."[146]
Not only had the American ambassador to Tel Aviv
made "serious representations" to Mrs. Meir
immediately after the Israeli cease-fire violation, but according to Moshe Dayan:

> The Americans, in order to smooth
> the way with the Arabs, confronted
> us with an ultimatum to the effect
> that, if we would not enable the
> Third Army to receive food and
> water, we would find ourselves in
> a political conflict with them
> (the Americans) . . .[147]

Dayan further charged that the US had threatened
to fly supplies to relieve the encircled Third
Army if Israel refused to allow food and water
through the lines.

In view of the American interest in limiting
the success of the Israeli victory, it is at least
conceivable that Kissinger put American forces on
alert, in part at least, to send a signal to Tel
Aviv (not only to show the American concern over
the fate of the Third Army, but also to tell the

Israelis that the US had an interest in containing the advance of Israeli troops). If this explanation of the alert is, indeed, true, it raises serious questions over the acceptability of US-Israeli relations. It is entirely unacceptable for a nation to be forced into avoidable confrontations merely to convincingly communicate to an "ally" the need for cooperation on central issues (like the observance or non-observance of a cease-fire). In any event, the wisdom of such a policy (running the risk of provoking a nuclear confrontation as a device for extracting cooperation from a non-nuclear client nation) is open to considerable criticism.

A related possible intention of the US military alert was to communicate to Israel the real danger of a major confrontation between the United States and the Soviet Union over the Middle East. The alert may have been intended to impress upon the Israelis that if they continued to refuse relief to reach the encircled Egyptian Third Army, the Soviet Union would militarily intervene on behalf of the Arabs, which could lead in turn to a superpower confrontation. But whether this or some other motive was behind the decision to place American military forces on alert, the fact remains that the position of the surrounded Egyptian forces improved dramatically immediately after the alert. This does not prove a causal relationship, but it does make it harder to assess the appropriateness of what was clearly a dangerous policy that might have precipitated a serious confrontation with the Soviet Union. Whether the international situation actually justified such risks is, perhaps, impossible to determine definitively.

However, Kissinger's decision was also based on domestic political considerations. Immediately after the alert there was speculation that the president's "flourish of crisis diplomacy" was a device to divert attention from his domestic political troubles. According to Newsweek, an unnamed administration aide openly admitted that "we had a problem, and we decided to make the most of it"[148] A similar line of argument was reported in the Washington Post, which in its issue of 25 October stated that despite the bipartisan support for the President's warning to the Soviets, in private there was an "undercurrent of suspicion that the president might have escalated the crisis . . . to . . . take people's minds off his domestic problems."

Nevertheless, although Watergate was on the President's mind, the decision to place American forces on alert was made primarily by Kissinger and not Nixon. Of course, even Kissinger was concerned about Watergate and public opinion. But Kissinger's preoccupation with domestic politics went beyond Nixon's immediate political difficulties. He was concerned with the impact of domestic politics on American foreign policy. To understand his political philosophy. Probably the most revealing clue on this subject is Kissinger's reaction to the Cuban Missile Crisis. Immediately after Kennedy's confrontation with the Soviets in 1962, Kissinger, then a professor of government at Harvard University, argued that Moscow's decision to install missiles in Cuba had been based essentially on Soviet perceptions of American domestic politics. According to Kissinger:

> With the stakes so high, what made the Soviets believe they could get away with it? Over the past decade Khrushchev may well have become convinced that the United States would never run risks to protect its interests, either because it did not understand its interests or because it did not have the appropriate doctrine for using its power.[149]

In October 1973, the Watergate affair had effectively isolated the American presidency. There were reports about Nixon's role in the cover up and there were Congressional voices

urging his impeachment. Besides, Watergate
occurred in the immediate aftermath of the Vietnam
War. There was concern that, as a reaction to th
American entanglement in Southeast Asia, the United
States might return to a policy of isolationism.
Within the context of these considerations, Kissinger, both as a strategist and statesman, felt it
was necessary to indicate to the Soviets that even
in a situation of domestic difficulties the United
States had both the will and the power to guard its
international interests. As far as Kissinger was
concerned, the issues facing him during October
went beyond the fate of the Arabs and the Israelis.
For Kissinger, who viewed the Middle East conflict
preiminently in terms of Soviet-American rivalry,
the issue was not whether Moscow actually planned
to intervene in the Middle East. At stake was the
ability and willingness of the Americans to respond
to Soviet tactics of intimidation. Kissinger's
evaluation of the Cuban Missile Crises is indicative of his philosophy on this question:

> On October 22, President Kennedy
> boldly seized an opportunity given
> few statesmen: to change the course
> of events by one dramatic move.
> His action achieved far more than
> the immediate goal of dismantling
> Soviet missile bases in Cuba. It
> exploded the myth that in every
> situation the Soviets were prepared
> to run greater risks than we. This
> myth has been the basis of Soviet
> atomic blackmail and had trans-
> formed too many conferences into
> opportunities for the Soviets to
> set the terms of negotiations.[150]

Thus, in October 1973, Kissinger put the American military on a nuclear alert not necessarily
or exclusively because he thought there was a
strong possibility of a military confrontation,
but rather to demonstrate to the Soviets that the
US was prepared to take risks when it deemed it
necessary. With or without Watergate, the Soviets

would not be permitted to gain advantage through
intimidation.

The alert, therefore, was based in part it
would seem on political considerations. The
probability of a military confrontation may not
have been high, at least not as high as during the
civil war in Jordan. The alert also seems to have
been directed at both the Soviets and the Israelis.
With the Soviets, however, the alert was intended
to reflect an overall American posture of will and
power. It did not indicate that the American
policy was in strict conflict with the Soviets.
Both powers shared the same objective: to save the
Arabs. It was only the approaches that differed.

The American nuclear alert did not last long.
By late 26 October, the alert for the Strategic
Air Command and the North American Air Defense was
relaxed. By the following day, American forces
were put back on Defense Condition Four, the normal
status of American troops.

The "success" of policies like the US nuclear
alert that are supposedly aimed at deterring an
adversary from a specific course of action are
virtually impossible to evaluate. First, in the
present case it would be necessary to demonstrate
that affecting Soviet behavior actually was the
primary objective of the alert (and not domestic
political considerations). Second, it would have
to be convincingly demonstrated that Soviet intervention would have taken place in the absence of
such an alert. Our discussion suggests that
neither of these conditions can be met in analyzing
the American nuclear alert.

All that can be stated with certainty is that
a major confrontation between the US and the
Soviet Union did not develop. Whether this was
because the US succeeded in convincing the Soviets
of its will and determination, or because the
Soviets never seriously intended to intervene in
the Middle East is impossible to establish. We do

know that the USSR's criticism of the US alert
was rather low keyed and that there was no
general perception that the US had succeeded in
forcing the Soviets to "back down" as it had in
the Cuban confrontation. Rather, the Soviet Union
attributed the US alert to an effort by the Nixon
Administration to "distract the country from the
domestic difficulties."[151] We also know that
immediately following the alert the US and the
USSR were both able to accept a Security Council
resolution excluding both Superpowers from partici-
pating in any peace-keeping operations in the
Middle East. (The Security Council authorized
the Secretary General to use forces from Austria,
Finland, and Sweden to supervise the cease-fire).
Thus, the Soviet Union also achieved its <u>stated</u>
purposes (the rescue of the Third Army and the
effective enforcement of the cease-fire) as much
as the US achieved its <u>stated</u> objective (preventing
Soviet military involvement in the Middle East.)

A useful conclusion that arises out of this
investigation is that Superpower confrontations
can be either zero-sum contest (as in Cuba) or
sum-sum contests (as in the October War.) Kissinger might claim that his willingness to go to the
brink of nuclear war succeeded in dissuading the
Soviets from establishing a military presence in
the Middle East. But a Soviet claim that its
willingness to unilaterally intervene succeeded in
gaining the effective implementation of the cease-
fire would have just as much credibility.

Peace Efforts

After saving the Third Army, at least tem-
porarily, Kissinger devoted his entire time to
stabilizing the cease-fire. This required a quick
disengagement of military forces. The task was
difficult, and required several trips to the
Middle East, but by late January 1974, Israel and
Egypt had reached an agreement.[152] The disengagement accord provided for the withdrawal of Israeli

forces from the wast bank of the canal and the pull-
back of all Israeli forces to a point twenty miles
into the Sinai. The twenty miles on the east
bank was divided into three zones: two limited
forces areas, one for each side, separated by a
buffer zone. In the limited force zones, which
were five to seven and one-half miles wide, each
side was allowed to station a maximum of seven
thousand troops. The buffer zone, three and a half
to five miles deep, was placed under United Nation
control.

The Israeli-Egyptian agreement eased the Middle
Eastern political-military climate considerably.
But the lack of an agreement between Syria and
Israel kept the overall situation volatile. It
took several months of intensive diplomatic effort
by Kissinger before an agreement was reached on
the eastern front. Indeed, in the last phase of
negotiations, it took Kissinger twenty-seven days
of "shuttle diplomacy" between Damascus and Jerusalem before a disengagement agreement between
Syria and Israel was signed late in May 1974.[153]
The agreement was patterned after the Egyptian-
Israeli disengagement pact. According to its terms,
Israel withdrew from the entire territory captured
in October and a few strips of land conquered in
1967. A buffer zone was created and put under UN
control. On either side of this zone were militarily thinned-out zones. Each side was permitted
to station a maximum of six thousand troops,
seventy-five tanks, and thirty-six short range
cannons in their respective zones. Finally, the
agreement provided for the exchange of prisoners
between both sides.

The outcome of the October War served as a
turning point in Middle Eastern politics. It
facilitated further negotiations between Egypt and
Israel leading to the March 1979 Washington Agreement (the Camp David Accords) between the two
countries. Furthermore, Kissinger's success in
his diplomatic efforts in the Middle East increased
American prestige in the Arab world. After almost
a decade of tension between the US and Egypt,

relations were normalized. And by the end of 1974, American diplomatic relations had been restored with many other Arab countries.

The Oil Factor and US Foreign Policy

A major consequence of the October War was the initiation of the so-called energy crisis in the United States as a result of the Arab oil embargo. Throughout 1973, the Saudis had threatened to use oil as an economic weapon against the US if Washington did not reverse its pro-Israeli position.[154] In an interview with Richard Hunt of the National Broadcasting Company in late Summer 1973, Saudi Arabia's King Faisal stated that:

> We do not wish to place any
> restriction on our oil export to the
> United States, but, as I mentioned,
> America's complete support of
> Zionism against the Arabs makes
> it extremely difficult for us to
> continue to supply the United
> States' petroleum needs and to
> even maintain our friendly rela-
> tions with the United States.[155]

But despite this and various other warning, the Nixon Administration did not give much consideration to Faisal's threats. The typical American reaction to the Saudi's warning in 1973 was that the Arabs should not be taken seriously; for after all, "the Arabs could not drink their oil." The fact that the Arabs had tried but failed to impose an oil embargo against the US in 1967 gave even less credibility to the Arab threats in 1973. Thus, when during the October War the Saudis and the other Arab oil-producing countries actually did reduce oil production, many officials in the US government were caught completely by surprise.[156]

The Arab decision to cut oil production came a day after the announcement by the Nixon Adminis-

tration of a $2.2 billion aid package for Israel.
On 17 October, the Organization of Arab Petroleum
Exporting Countries (OAPEC) announced a five
percent cutback in its oil production. The cutback was to increase by five percent every month [157]
until Israel withdrew from occupied territories.
Furthermore, on the same day (17 October), the six
largest Persian Gulf oil-producing countries
announced a seventeen percent increase in the price
of their crude oil and a seventy percent increase
in taxes to be paid by foreign oil produced and
sold by the companies.

The cutback in production and increase in
price was followed by still another important
move. On 20 October, the government of Saudi
Arabia announced that "in view of the increase in
American military aid to Israel, the Kingdom of
Saudi Arabia has decided to halt oil export to the
United States of America . . ." [158] The Arab
embargo against the United States became total
when Kuwait, Bahrain, Qatar, and Dubai announced
similar halts in shipments of oil and petroleum
products to the US the next day.

The oil embargo against the US was lifted in
March 1974, in response to Kissinger's efforts to
mediate the Arab-Israeli conflict. But the oil
embargo, the production cutback, and the price
increase precipitated an energy cirsis in the US
whose effects lasted through 1974, and which has
remained an important domestic issue ever since.

The oil crisis in the United States was
manifested in sky-rocketing gasoline and crude
oil prices, and in long lines at service stations
throughout the country. Various short- and long-
term plans were prepared including the rationing
of gasoline. But by late 1974, the supply situation had returned to normal with a number of
important economic side effects. First, the
prices of gasoline and other petroleum products
were never returned to their earlier levels.
Second, the energy crisis "weakened the American
environmental movement in the energy area," result-

ing in the expansion of the offshore drilling and construction of nuclear power plants.[159]

Far more serious, the oil embargo revealed the increasing dependence of the US on imported oil. As late as 1970 members of the American academic community could argue that:

> Middle Eastern petroleum, which is by far the largest /US foreign investment_/ income earner, is the one product on which the United States is not dependent. The American source is domestic and Latin American. In the future it probably will be Alaskan and Rocky Mountain.[160]

In point of fact, at the time of the Arab oil embargo, the US imported roughly one-third of its petroleum needs. The embargo interupted approximately 30 percent of US foreign supplies, meaning that total supply in the US was reduced by around 10%.[161] Still, as David Howard Davis has observed, "The American reaction approached panic."[162] Be that as it may, the United States continued to increase its consumption of foreign (and especially Middle Eastern) oil in the following years. By 1979, over half the nation's petroleum needs were supplied by imports, and the percentage of petroleum imports coming from the Arab world had increased dramatically.[163] Accordingly, Under Secretary of State, Warren Christopher warned in Mid-1979 that:

> Our country has an awesome dependence on foreign oil at a time when the supply is running out. This massive dependence on foreign oil is jeopardizing our national security and our economic prosperity.[164]

Although the international energy crisis was, perhaps, inevitable in terms of the simple dynamics of supply and demand (world consumption had been increasing at about five percent per annum for several decades)[165] US policies during the October War indisputably exacerbated the situation.

A related issue is the conduct of US oil companies in the embargo. It is outside the scope of this study to fully review the role of American oil companies in the oil crisis of 1973. It is also outside the realm of our investigation to examine the total impact of American oil companies on US foreign policy.[166] However, some general remarks about the influence of the oil companies on the US policy toward the Arab-Israeli conflict seem helpful at this juncture.

In general, while the oil companies were influential in the formation of American policy toward such non-Arab countries as Iran, they were less preoccupied with US policy toward the Arab-Israeli conflict prior to 1973. According to William Quandt:

> Compared to the influence of the American Jewish community, that of American oil companies is slight. Whatever their behavior on matters of domestic policics, the oil companies have usually been cautious in trying to determine American policy on the Arab-Israeli question. Their opinions are generally heard and are often solicited, but virtually no intensive efforts to alter US policies on the Middle East have been from the oil companies.[167]

Furthermore, Quandt has observed that:

> Within the government . . . there is general agreement that the oil companies are not very high powered in their efforts to influence policy

on the Arab-Israeli conflict.
Oil company executives similarly
stress their lack of effectiveness on Arab-Israeli matters.[168]

There are two central reasons for the relatively
low involvement of the oil companies in the Arab-
Israeli conflict prior to 1973. First, American
oil companies were "sensitive to the dangers of
displeasing American Jewish opinion by seeming to
be anti-Israeli."[169] Second, and more important,
was the fact that prior to the early 1970s American oil interests were not threatened by the Arab-
Israeli conflict. Due to the animosity between
Nasser and the government of Saudi Arabia, where
most American oil interests were located, the
Saudis were not willing to use their oil as a pol-
itical-economic weapon to further the cause of
Egypt.

There were three areas of conflict between
Egypt and Saudi Arabia. First, the Saudis never
showed any receptivity toward Nasser's Pan-Arabism,
for at the heart of the Nasser design was a unified
Arab world dominated by Cairo. Second, the Saudis
were concerned over Nasser's close ties with Moscow,
fearing that this would facilitate the growth of
communism in the Middle East. And, finally, the
Egyptian support of the Republican forces during
the Yemeni civil war in the 1960's, while the
Saudis were assisting the monarchy, created considerable cleavage between Riyadh and Cairo. (Between 1962-1967, Cairo sent as many as 30,000
troops into Yemeni to support the Republican
forces). The oil factor was thus left out of the
Arab-Israeli equation prior to 1973. The clearest
expression of this view was Faisal's statement in
1967 that "oil and politics do not mix."[170]

The death of Nasser in fall 1970, however,
changed Faisal's position on the use of oil as a
weapon. Replacement of Nasser by a moderate
Sadat resulted in improved Saudi-Egyptian relations.[171] As a result, by early 1973, Faisal was

65

prepared to use his oil in order to affect the
outcome of the Arab-Israeli conflict, and he
informed the Americans of his intentions.[172]   However, even then the US did not respond to Faisal's
threat of an oil embargo. Not only was Faisal's
threat disregarded for reasons of credibility, but
"the US did not feel that it could afford to put
itself in the position of pressuring Israel for
concessions in obvious response to King Faisal's
oil threat."[173]   Within the context of strong
support for Israel in the US, "this would be, to
say the least, bad politics."[174]

        After the Arabs demonstrated their ability to
use oil effectively as a political weapon, Washington decision-makers were forced to give more
consideration to the demands of the Arab world.
The 1973 oil embargo hurt the United States in two
ways. First, it had a direct impact on American
consumers as already noted. At the time of the
embargo, at least 25.6 percent of America's imported
oil came from Arab producers, which in turn
accounted for just over ten percent of total
American consumption.[175]   Thus, the embargo reduced
oil supplies in the US enough to cause spot short-
ages and soaring prices, but it did not cripple the
American economy much less the business interests
of the leading oil companies. To put the matter
bluntly, the Arab oil embargo reduced the sales of
US oil companies by about 10 percent, but increased
profits on the remaining 90 percent more than
enough to make the entire affair a windfall for
these corporations. If any single corporate
group in the US benefited from the embargo, it
was the major oil companies. The second, and more
important, effect of the oil embargo was the strain
it placed on US relations with Western Europe and
Japan. In 1973, Western Europe and Japan depended
on Arab oil production for 69.7 and 44.3 percent of
their consumption, respectively.[176]   It was the
dependence of these US allies on Arab oil that made
the embargo effective. And it was the fact that
unilateral US policies were responsible for the
disruption of oil flows to Western Europe and Japan

that strained their relations with Washington, since they were in effect experiencing the repercussion of policies in which they had had no voice.

Oil has remained an important, perhaps the most important, political issue since the October War. The ability of the Arab oil producing countries to effectively control the flow of oil to the developed capitalist countries which was demonstrated in 1973 (previous embargos had always failed) gave rise to a world-wide oil cartel, OPEC. The dependency of Western nations on a few large oil producers has permitted OPEC nations to set their own price for oil, causing permanent transformations in the economies of developed countries which had become accustomed to cheap energy. Yet at the time of the Arab-Israeli conflict in 1973 there had existed very little concern in Washington that America's one-sided support for Israel might have any direct or lasting effect on the American economy.

Conclusions

Our review of US involvement in the October War has revealed a number of interesting insights into the process by which American foreign policy is formulated and executed. The first point which should be emphasized is that it seems evident that the US missed an opportunity to avert war in the region by its failure to appreciate the significance of the split between Cairo and Moscow, its inability to understand the political pressures that might force Sadat into a war regardless of purely military considerations, and the unwillingness of the US to press for concessions from Israel. This last point deserves stressing. Events before, during and after the October War reveal that US policy toward the Middle East was dictated as much by the Jewish government as by Washington. The Jewish lobby in the US has proven to be extraordinarily strong, and virtually without any effective counter weight until the question of oil became salient after the October War.

The failure of both the US and Israel to detect the approach of war can be attributed to two things: a breakdown in intelligence and the complacency of decision-makers. Our conclusion is that the second factor was far more significant than the first. In spite of sophisticated US intelligence gathering equipment, including satellite surveillance, and the Israelis reputation for efficiency and accuracy, the intelligence arms of both countries failed to detect the approach of war until only a matter of hours before the outbreak of hostilities.[177] But a large part of intelligence concerns the analysis and interpretation of data, and this is where the assumptions of leaders became crucial. Both American and Israeli leaders over emphasized the importance of military strength as a determinant of a country's foreign policy. Such a view is consistent with the "realist" theory of international relations. Since the Arabs had suffered a devastating defeat in the Six-Day War in 1967 from which they had not yet completely recovered in 1973, the US and Israel refused to consider the possibility of war seriously. In short, they believed that a "considerable period of time would elapse before the Arabs would be ready for war."[178] As Moshe Dayan remarked before the Israeli Defense Forces staff college on 10 August 1973, "The balance of forces is so much in our favor that it neutralizes the Arab considerations and motives for the immediate renewal of hostilities."[179]

Within the context of such assumptions, the tendency was to discount or ignore intelligence data that pointed toward an Arab attack. For example, although Israel obtained hard evidence of Egyptian troop concentrations on the west bank of the Suez Canal, intelligence analysts assessed the probability of an Arab attack as "low" to "remote."[180] The primary difficulty with the US and Israeli focus on military considerations is that it overlooked the fact that the initiation of war is an essentially political decision, and is therefore subject to political determinants as much as it is purely military considerations.

Often in history wars are fought not by rational generals, but by frustrated leaders. And by 1973, Sadat was such a leader. The Egyptian economy was then under an almost intolerable strain. According to Mohammed Heikal:

> Industrial development, the High Dam, and the burden of war in the Yemen had made the early and middle sixties a period of extreme difficulty. Then had come the 1967 defeat and the need for an almost complete rebuilding and re-equipping of the army. In five years--between 1968 and 1973-- Egypt spent $8-$9 billion on the war effort. For the Egyptian people it had been a decade of sacrifice and austerity, such as no people could be expected to put up with indefinitely.[181]

From a political point of view, the situation was worse. There had been increasing demonstrations in Egypt beginning in 1971.[182] Although the demonstrations were anti-Sadat, the roots of the opposition went beyond hostility to the Sadat government. The credibility of the whole regime was in question. The explanation was simple. As de Gaulle once noted, "Any regime which fails to protect the frontiers of the nation, automatically loses its legitimacy."[183] Both the Six-Day War and the War of Attrition had proven that the leaders in Cairo could not protect their citizens from Israeli agressions. What made the situation even worse was Sadat's own rhetoric. Throughout 1971, he had spoken of "the year of decision." Two years passed, and the situation remained the same. There was no "decision." As a result, Sadat created a credibility gap for himself; not only in Egypt, but in the Arab world as a whole.

Thus, war became a political "necessity for Sadat's regime."[184]

According to Heikal:

> By 1973 Egypt had almost become the laughing stock of the Arab world. We claimed to be the leader and protector of the Arabs, but gave no lead to our own people and showed ourselves unable to protect our own territory.[185]

Insofar as US involvement in the war itself is concerned, both the airlift of military supplies to Israel and the subsequent nuclear alert reveal the cross pressures that exist within the policy making and execution process. Our discussion demonstrated that there were at least three possible explanations for the lag between the initial US decision to resupply Israel and the actual beginning of the airlift. Regardless of which of the explanations is the most accurate, certain facts stand out--specifically, that there was less than perfect cooperation between two important branches of the foreign policy establishment (State and Defense); that even after the apparent decision to resupply Israel it was possible for some individuals to delay the implementation of the policy by raising issues about methods (whose plans should be used in the airlift?); and that although the US and Israel were close allies, it was necessary for the Israeli Ambassador to apply political pressure on the Nixon Administration to achieve the desired results (the threat to mobilize Jewish support in Congress). If nothing else, the airlift decision demonstrates the bureaucratic context of policy implementation, and the significant (and sometimes decisive) role that personality (Kissinger's and Schlesinger's) can play within that context.

The decision to place American military forces on alert in response to an apparent or perceived Soviet threat to intervene in the Middle East illustrates another facet of the foreign policy process. First, it shows that brinkmanship (the willingness to go to the very brink of full scale war in order to communicate opposition to an opponent's actions) remains an intrinsic element in Soviet-American relations. And it reminds us how quickly conflicts involving other parties can escalate into Superpower confrontations, even in an era of supposed détente.

Second, the fact that the US alert did not damage Soviet-American relations suggests that conflict and cooperation are not mutually exclusive, but rather intimately intertwined in international relations. The fact that one day the United States could consider nuclear war against the Soviet Union, and the next day resume the myriad of mutually advantageous interactions that take place between the two countries shows that conflict and cooperation are both present at the same time in Superpower relations.

Third, the difficulty in establishing the actual motives that were behind the nuclear alert (domestic political considerations, actual fear of Soviet intervention, or to place pressure on the Israelis) demonstrates how many widely separate considerations can be brought to bear on any single foreign policy action. In all probability, all three factors figured into the decision to place American forces on Alert, and not simply the threat of Soviet intervention as Kissinger has claimed. The reality is that major foreign policy outputs are more often the products of a whole set of considerations than they are automatic reflexes to singular external events. In other words, it is not difficult to appreciate that the nuclear alert would have been significantly less probable had officials anticipated an adverse public reaction. The myth that domestic politics stops at the point where foreign policy and national security begin is just that, a myth.

Notes

1. For an early analysis see Anthony McDermott, "A Russian Withdrawal; or Divorce, Egyptian Style," The New Middle East, no. 47 (August 1972), pp. 4-6.

2. See Mohamed Heikal, The Road to Ramadan (N.Y.: Ballantine Books, 1975), p. 175.

3. Ibid., pp. 168-169.

4. Jon D. Glassman, Arms for the Arabs: The Soviet Union and War in the Middle East (Baltimore: The Johns Hopkins University Press, 1975), p. 94.

5. Walter Laqueur, Confrontation: The Middle East and World Politics (N.Y.: Bantam Books, 1974), p. 18.

6. "Speech by President Sadat of Egypt Reviewing U.S.S.R.-Egypt Relations, Made on the Twentieth Anniversary of the July Revolution," International Documents on Palestine, 1972, ed. Jorgen S. Nielsen (Beirut: The Institute for Palestine Studies, 1975), p. 335.

7. McDermott, "A Russian Withdrawal," p. 6.

8. Robert W. Stookey, America and the Arab States: An Uneasy Encounter (N.Y.: John Wiley and Sons, Inc., 1975), p. 243; The Insight Team of the London Sunday Times, The Yom Kippur War (N.Y.: Doubleday and Co., Inc., 1974), p. 58.

9. U.S. Congress, House Committee on Foreign Relations, Subcommittee on the Near East, Congressmen Visit Israel and Egypt (Washington, D.C.: Government Printing Office, 1972), p. 17.

10. Lawrence L. Whetten, The Canal War: Four-Power Conflict in the Middle East (Cambridge, Mass.: The MIT Press, 1974), p. 233.

11. Marvin Kalb and Bernard L. Kalb, Kissinger (Boston: Little, Brown and Co., 1974), p. 451.

12. Cited in John G. Stoessinger, Henry Kissinger: The Anguish of Power (N.Y.: W. W. Norton and Co., Inc., 1976), p. 41.

13. Cited in Middle East Research and Information Project, no. 22 (November 1973), p. 20.

14. Whetten, The Canal War, p. 235.

15. Heikal, The Road to Ramadan, pp. 38-48; Elizabeth Monroe and A. H. Farr-Hockley, The Arab, Israel War, October 1973: Background and Events, Adelphi Papers, no. 11 (Winter 1974-1975), p. 5.

16. Whetten, The Canal War, pp. 234-235.

17. New York Times, 14 March 1973.

18. Stookey, America and the Arab States, p. 243.

19. The Sunday Times, 14 October 1973.

20. For details see John Bulloch, The Making of a War: The Middle East from 1967 to 1973 (London: Longman Group Ltd, 1974), pp. 17-30.

21. There are a variety of names for this war: The October War, the Yom Kippur War, and the Ramadan War. Throughout this work these names will be used interchangeably. The fourth Arab-Israeli war has generated a

burgeoning body of literature. The following are among the general works on the subject: Nasser H. Aruri, ed., Middle East Crucible: Studies on the Arab-Israeli War of October 1973 (Illinois: The Medina University Press International, 1975); Bulloch, The Making of a War; Golia Golan, Yom Kippur and After: The Soviet Union and the Middle East Crisis (Cambridge: Cambridge University Press, 1976; _____, The Soviet Union and the Arab-Israel War of October 1973; Jerusalem Papers on Peace Problems, no. 7 (June 1974); Heikal, The Road to Ramadan; Cham Herzog, The War of Atonement: October, 1973 (Boston: Little, Brown and Co., 1975); The Insight Team, The Yom Kippur War; Laqueur, Confrontation; Malcolm Mackintosh et al., The Middle East and the International System: The Impact of the 1973 War, Adelphi Papers, no. 114 (September 1974); Harvey Sicherman, The Yom Kippur War: End of Illusion?, Foreign Policy Papers, vol. 1 no. 4 (1976).

The chronology that follows is based upon the following sources: Report on World Affairs 54 (July to December 1973):30-34; and Lester A. Sobel, ed., Israel and the Arabs: The October 1973 War (N.Y.: Facts on File, Inc., 1974).

22. See Sobel, Israel and the Arabs, p. 107; The Insight Team, The Yom Kippur War, p. 391.

23. For the text of this resolution see U.S. Congress, Senate Committee on Foreign Relations, A Select Chronology and Background Documents Relating to the Middle East, 2nd rev. ed., 94th Cong., 1st sess., 1975, p. 285.

24. For the text of these two resolutions see Ibid., p. 286.

25. Kalb and Kalb, Kissinger, p. 450.

26. See for example Ibid., p. 455; The Insight
    Team, The Yom Kippur War, pp. 91-92. For
    details on the Israeli perception regarding
    Arabs' war plans and capability see Avi
    Shlaim, "Failures in National Intelligence
    Estimate: The Case of the Yom Kippur War,"
    World Politics 28 (April 1976); Amos Perl-
    Mutter, "Israel's Fourth War, October 1973:
    Political and Military Misperception,"
    Orbis 19 (Summer 1975):434-460; Abraham Ben-
    Zvi, "Misperceiving the Role of Perception:
    A Critique," The Jerusalem Journal of Inter-
    national Relations 2 (Winter 1976-1977):74-
    91; _____, "Hindsight and Foresight: A
    Conceptual Framework for the Analysis of
    Surprise Attacks," World Politics 28 (April
    1976):381-395; S. Z. Abramov, "The Agranat
    Report and its Aftermath," Midstream 29
    (June/July 1974):16-28; Michael Handel,
    Perception, Deception and Surprise: The
    Case of the Yom Kippur War, Jerusalem Papers
    on Peace Problems, no. 19. Also see Herzog,
    The War of Atonement, pp. 40-55; The Insight
    Team, The Yom Kippur War, pp. 90-113; and
    Haim Var Lev, "Surprise in the Yom Kippur
    War," Military Aspects of the Israeli-Arab
    War, pp. 259-265.

27. Kalb and Kalb, Kissinger, p. 456; Laqueur,
    Confrontation, p. 163; also see "Secretary
    Kissinger's News Conference of October 25,"
    Department of State Bulletin 69 (12 November
    1973):585-594, esp. p. 585 and Stoessinger,
    Kissinger, p. 179. Some analysts have
    argued that the terrorist action in Austria
    was part of Arab's strategy to deceive Israel.
    See Shlaim, "Failures in National Intelli-
    gence," p. 355.

28. Kalb and Kalb, Kissinger, p. 456; Stoessinger,
    Kissinger, p. 179.

29. Tad Szulc, "Seeing and not believing," The
    New Republic, 22 December 1973, p. 13; also

see Shlaim, "Failures in National Intelligence," p. 360; The Insight Team, The Yom Kippur War, pp. 91-113.

30. Szulc,"Seeing and not Believing," p. 14.

31. Newsweek, 9 April 1973, pp. 44-45.

32. Herzog, The War of Atonement, p. 25.

33. Sicherman, The Yom Kippur War, p. 32. This mobilization cost $11 million. Thus, in October, in the hours immediately prior to the outbreak of war, some Israelis were hesitant to call another mobilization fearing that they might be criticized if the Arab attack did not occur. See Shlaim, "Failures in National Intelligence," p. 359.

34. See for example Coral Bell, "The October Middle East War: A Case Study in Crisis Management During Détente," International Affairs (London) 50 (October 1974):531-543; Golan, Yom Kippur and After; Foy D. Kohler, Leon Gouri and Mose L. Harvey, The Soviet Union and the October 1973 Middle East War: The Implications for Détente (Miami: The University of Miami, 1974); Marshal D. Shulman, "Strategic Forum: The Middle East Conflict--1973," Survival 16 (January and February 1974):3-5.

35. Foreign Broadcast Information Service/Egypt, 16 September 1975, pp. D4-D5.

36. Alvin Rubenstein, Red Star on the Nile: The Soviet-Egyptian Influence Relationship Since the June War (Princeton, N.J.: Princeton University Press, 1977), p. 262.

37. Lucius D. Battle, "Peace-Inshullah," Foreign Policy, no. 14 (Spring 1974), p. 122.

38. Rubenstein, Red Star, p. 254.

39. _Ibid._, p. 259.

40. The Israelis have implied that they were
    aware of an impending war. But due to
    pressure from Kissinger, who had warned them
    against a pre-emptive attack, they did not
    strike first. See,Golda Meir, _My Life_
    (Dell Publishing Co., In., Inc., 1975), p. 411;
    Kalb and Kalb, _Kissinger_, p. 460. To this
    charge Kissinger replied in his news confer-
    ence of 26 October:
    > I mention this personal detail because
    > it answers the question that the
    > United States intervention prevented
    > Israel from taking pre-emptive action
    > (as implied by Prime Minister Golda
    > Meir on October 6 and 13). The
    > United States made no demarche to
    > either side before October 6, because
    > all the intelligence given us by
    > foreign countries suggested that
    > there was no possibility of the
    > outbreak of war.
    "Secretary Kissinger's News Conference of
    October 25," _Department of State Bulletin_
    69 (12 November 1973):585.

41. Kohler, Goure, and Harvey, _The Soviet Union_,
    p. 90.

42. Stoessinger, _Kissinger_, p. 186.

43. The most authoritative pro-Kissinger
    account is given in Kalb and Kalb, _Kissinger_,
    pp. 461-478; also see Stoessinger, _Kissinger_,
    pp. 180-187.

44. Kalb and Kalb, _Kissinger_, p. 464.

45. _Ibid._, p. 465.

46. _Ibid._

47. _Ibid._, p. 465.

48. Ibid., p. 467.

49. Ibid.

50. Ibid.

51. Ibid., p. 469.

52. Ibid., p. 471.

53. Ibid.

54. Ibid., p. 472.

55. Ibid.

56. Ibid., p. 475.

57. Ibid., p. 477.

58. Ibid.

59. For the details on the quantity of arms
     supplied to Israel during this period, see
     Aviation Week and Space Technology 99 (10 Dec-
     ember 1973):16-19; also see Edmund Ghareeb,
     "The U.S. Arms Supply to Israel During the
     War," Journal of Palestine Studies 3 (Winter
     1974):114-121.

60. The anti-Kissinger version has been publicized
     in the following works: Matti Golan, The
     Secret Conversations of Henry Kissinger:
     Step-by-Step Diplomacy in the Middle East
     (New York: Quadrangle/The New York Times
     Book Co., 1976), pp. 33-62; Gil Carl AlRoy,
     The Kissinger Experience: American Policy in
     the Middle East (New York: Horizon Press,
     1975), pp. 69-84; Edward R. F. Sheehan, The
     Arabs, Israelis, and Kissinger: A Secret
     History of American Diplomacy in the Middle
     East (New York: Reader's Digest Press, 1976),
     pp. 33-39; Edward N. Luttwak and Walter
     Laqueur, "Kissinger and the Yom Kippur War,"
     Commentary 58 (September 1974):33-40; Tad

Szulc, "Is He Indispensable? Answers to the Kissinger Riddle," New York, 1 July 1974, pp. 33-39.

61. Quandt, Decade of Decisions, pp. 170-176.

62. For an analysis of the role of the reserve units in Israel's military see Laqueur, Confrontation, p. 93.

63. Matti Golan, The Secret Conversations, p. 46.

64. See for example Sobel, ed., Israel and the Arabs, p. 86.

65. Senator Fulbright, the chairman of the Senate's influential Committee on Foreign Relations, told a reporter on CBS's Face the Nation early in October that: "Israel controls the policy in the Congress . . . the emotional and political ties are too strong . . . . On every test on anything the Israelis are interested in the Senate . . . the Israelis have seventy-five to eighty votes." Cited in Near East Report 17 (10 October 1973):162.

66. Szulc, "Is He Indispensable?," p. 37.

67. Sheehan, The Arabs, Israelis, and Kissinger, p. 32.

68. Laqueur and Luttwak, "Kissinger and the Yom Kippur War," p. 39.

69. Some officials in Washington feared that their close association with the Israelis could have given rise to another surge of anti-Americanism in the Middle East. Furthermore, there was apprehension about the possibility of an oil embargo. Throughout summer 1973, the Arab governments (including the pro-American Saudis) had warned the U.S. that American military aid to Israel would result in an oil embargo.

According to Quandt, the reason behind the delay in the air lift was "to induce the Israelis to accept a cease-fire-in-place and in the conviction that the fighting was nearly over in any case." Decade of Decisions, p. 179.

70. Stoessinger, Kissinger.

71. Kalb and Kalb, Kissinger, p. 470.

72. Whetten, The Canal War, p. 284.

73. Kalb and Kalb, Kissinger, p. 462.

74. For details see Quandt, Decade of Decisions, pp. 170-183.

75. Golan, Yom Kippur and After, p. 65.

76. The Insight Team, The Yom Kippur War, p. 367.

77. Golan, Yom Kippur and After, p. 65.

78. Ibid.

79. Matti Golan, The Secret Conversations, pp. 66-67; also see Quandt, Decade of Decisions, pp. 181-182.

80. Bell, "The October Middle East War," pp. 531-543; and Abraham S. Becker, The Superpowers in the Arab-Israeli Conflict, 1970-1973, Rand Paper, p. 5167, December 1973, p. 2.

81. Golan, Yom Kippur and After, p. 108.

82. This resolution, adopted on 22 November 1967, by the Security Council, called for the withdrawal of Israeli armed forces from territories occupied in the Six-Day War.

83. See Heikal, The Road to Ramadan, p. 236.

84. See Golan, Yom Kippur and After, p. 112.

85. Kalb and Kalb, Kissinger, p. 481.

86. Ibid.

87. Quandt, The Decade of Decisions, pp. 190-191.

88. Matti Golan, The Secret Conversations, p. 75.

89. Kalb and Kalb, Kissinger, p. 485.

90. Ibid., p. 484.

91. For details on domestic political developments during this period, see Theodore White, Breach of Faith (New York: Dell, 1975), pp. 328-342.

92. For the text of this agreement see Mason Willrich and John B. Rhinelander, eds., SALT: The Moscow Agreements and Beyond (N.Y.: The Free Press, 1974), p. 278ff.

93. King Faisal of Saudi Arabia announced his decision one day after the U.S. Congress approved a bill providing for $2.2 billion in military aid to Israel. For details on this bill see U.S. Senate, Emergency Military Assistance for Israel and Cambodia, Hearings before the Committee on Foreign Relations, 93rd Cong., 1st sess., October 1973.

94. Quandt, Decade of Decisions, p. 190.

95. Beginning with the early 1970s, there appeared a number of articles in the U.S. which dealt with the problem of American dependence on foreign oil, particularly Middle Eastern oil. By October 1973, there was no agreement on the degree of U.S. dependence on the Arab's oil. See, for example, M. A. Adelman, "Is the Oil Shortage Real?," Foreign Policy, no. 9 (Winter 1972-1973), pp. 69-107; Jahangir

Amuzegar, "The Oil Story: Facts, Fiction,
and Fair Play," Foreign Affairs 51 (July
1973):676-689; Jean-Jacques Berreby, "Does
America Need Arab Oil," Survival 12 (June
1970), pp. 199-259; Walter Lacqueur and Edward
Luttwak, "Oil," Commentary 56 (October 1973):
37-43; Walter Levy, "Oil Power," Foreign
Affairs 49 (July 1971):652-668; U.S., Senate,
Energy and Foreign Policy, 93rd Cong., 1st
sess., 30 and 31 May 1973.

96. Kalb and Kalb, Kissinger, p. 485.

97. For the text of the resolution, see U.S.,
Senate, Committee on Foreign Realtions, A
Select Chronology and Background Documents
Relating to the Middle East, 2nd rev. ed.
(Washington, D.C.: Government Printing
Office, 1975), p. 285.

98. See The Insight Team, The Yom Kippur War,
p. 394.

99. Ibid., p. 398.

100. See Kalb and Kalb, Kissinger, p. 133.

101. Translated in Current Digest of Soviet Press
(C.D.S.P.) 25 (21 November 1973):7.

102. Kalb and Kalb, Kissinger, p. 490.

103. Soviet State in the Security Council on 24
October, cited in the Insight Team, The Yom
Kippur War, p. 404.

104. Ibid., p. 417; Laqueur, Confrontation, p. 201.

105. Kalb and Kalb, Kissinger, p. 487.

106. The Yom Kippur War, p. 399.

107. Matti Golan, The Secret Conversations, p. 86.
Emphasis added. Laqueur's account of Kissinger's meeting with the Israelis is very

82

similar to Golan's. See *Confrontation*, p. 197.

108. The Insight Team, *The Yom Kippur War*, p. 401.

109. Heikal, *The Road to Ramadan*, p. 257.

110. Cited in the Insight Team, *The Yom Kippur War*, p. 401.

111. Kalb and Kalb, *Kissinger*, p. 489.

112. A few hours after the receipt of Sadat's letter, the White House issued a statement refusing the request, expressing the hope that "other outside powers will not send troops to the Middle East." *New York Times*, 25 Ocotber, 1973.

113. Matti Golan, *The Secret Conversations*, p. 90.

114. Cited in Kalb and Kalb, *Kissinger*, p. 290. Part of this letter is quoted--without source-- in the International Institute for Strategic Studies, *Strategic Survey* 1973, p. 47; also see New York Times, 10 April 1974.

115. Cited without source in Golan, *Yom Kippur and After*, p. 122.

116. Kalb and Kalb, *Kissinger*, p. 490.

117. Cited in the Insight Team, *The Yom Kippur War*, p. 408. Prior to 1969, most of the N.S.C. meetings consisted of twenty-five participants. During the Nixon years, however, all major decisions regarding the Middle East were made by W.S.A.G., consisting of six or seven individuals which included: Kissinger, Schlesinger, Moorer, Deputy Secretary of State Kenneth Rush, Colby, Deputy Assistant Secretary of Defense for International Security Affairs James Noyes, and Deputy Assistant Secretary of State for the Near East Alfred Atherton.

118. There are five defense conditions in the U.S.
     military lexicon: 5. Forces not in state of
     readiness, troops lack training. 4. Normal
     peace time position as troops undergo train-
     ing. 3. Troops placed on standby and
     awaiting orders. All leaves cancelled. 2.
     Troops ready for combat. 1. Troops deployed
     for combat. The American military alert
     during the Cuban Missile Crisis was defense
     condition 2.

119. "Secretary Kissinger's News Conference of
     October 25," Department of State Bulletin
     69 (12 November 1973):589.

120. See The Insight Team, The Yom Kippur War, p.
     406, and Tad Szulc, "Is He Indispensable?
     Answers to the Kissinger Riddle," New York,
     1 July 1974, pp. 33-39.

121. The Insight Tea, The Yom Kippur War, p. 406.

122. Even Quandt's authoritative account is based
     entirely on the Kalbs' version. See Decade
     of Decisions, p. 196.

123. Ray S. Cline, "Policy without Intelligence,"
     Foreign Policy, no. 17 (Winter 1974-1975),
     p. 127. Also see Cline's statement in New
     York Times, 8 December 1974.

124. For a review of Soviet reaction see Pravda,
     28 and 29 October 1973, pp. 4 and 5 respec-
     tively. Translation in C.D.S.P. 55 (21 Nov-
     ember 1973): 7.

125. The Insight Team, The Yom Kippur War, p. 407.

126. Kalb and Kalb, Kissinger, p. 290.

127. "Secretary Kissinger's News Conference of
     October 25," Department of State Bulletin
     69 (12 November 1973):588.

128. "Secretary of Defense Schlesinger's News
     Conference," _Department of State Bulletin_
     69 (19 November 1973):617.

129. Cited without source in Golan, _Yom Kippur and
     After_, p. 122.

130. Tad Szulc, "Is He Indispensable? Answers to
     the Kissinger Riddle," p. 39.

131. Cline, "Policy without Intelligence," p. 133.
     Also see Cline's statement in _New York Times_,
     8 December 1974. Also see the report by
     Thomas Ross in _New York Post_, 5 November
     1974; Alroy, _The Kissinger Experience_, p. 78.
     Emphasis added.

132. Quandt, _Decade of Decisions_, pp. 196-197.

133. Golan, _The Yom Kippur War_, p. 122; Kalb and
     Kalb, _Kissinger_, p. 470. Also see "Schlesin-
     ger's News Conference of October 26," _Depart-
     ment of State Bulletin_ 69 (19 November 1973):
     623.

134. _Ibid._, p. 621.

135. See Kalb and Kalb, _Kissinger_, p. 493.

136. _Washington Post_, 22 November 1973. Also see
     Glassman, _Arms for the Arabs_, p. 163.

137. _New York Times_, 22 November 1973; also "Secre-
     tary Kissinger's News Conference of November
     21," _Department of State Bulletin_ 69 (10 Dec-
     ember 1973):703.

138. Rubinstein, _The Red Star_, p. 276.

139. "President Nixon's News Conference of Octo-
     ber 26," _Department of State Bulletin_ 69
     (12 November 1973):585.

140. AlRoy, _The Kissinger Experience_, p. 78.

141. "Secretary Kissinger's News Conference of
October 25," Department of State Bulletin
69 (12 November 1973):588.

142. Tad Szulc, "Why Kissinger's Time Is Up,"
New York, 14 April 1975, p. 39; AlRoy, The
Kissinger Experience, p. 82; Theodore
Draper, "The United States and Israel:
Tilt in the Middle East," Commentary 59
(April 1975):24-25. Dayan's account of events
does not indicate that the U.S. threatened
the Israelis; however, he does imply that the
Israelis came under severe pressure from
Kissinger after their encirclement of the
Egyptian Third Army. See Moshe Dayan,
Moshe Dayan: Story of My Life (New York:
Warner Books, 1977), pp. 660-661; also see,
Sheehan, The Arabs, Israelis, and Kissinger,
p. 38.

143. Ibid., p. 36.

144. Kalb and Kalb, Kissinger, p. 487.

145. "Why Kissinger's Time Is Up," p. 39.

146. AlRoy, Kissinger Experience, p. 82.

147. Terence Smith interview with Dayan in New
York Times, 26 January 1975; also see Dayan,
Moshe Dayan, pp. 660-661.

148. Newsweek, 5 November 1973.

149. "Reflections on Cuba," The Reporter 27
(22 November 1962):22.

150. Ibid., p. 21.

151. "Justified Skepticism," Pravda, 29 October
1973, p. 5; translated in C.D.S.P. 25 (November 1973):7.

152. For the text of this agreement see Committee
on Foreign Relations, A Select Chronology and

153. For the text of this agreement see Ibid.

154. John C. Campbell, "The Energy Crisis and
U.S. Policy in the Middle East," The Energy
Crisis and U.S. Foreign Policy, ed. Joseph
S. Szyliowicz and Bard E. O'Neill (N.Y.:
Praeger Publishers, 1975), p. 110.

155. For the text of this interview see Jorgen
S. Nielsen, ed., International Documents
on Palestine 1973 (Beirut: The Institute
for Palestine Studies, 1976), p. 451.

156. For details see Gerard J. Mangone, ed.,
Energy Policies of the World: Canada, China,
Arab States of the Persian Gulf, Venezuela,
Iran, vol. 1 (N.Y.: American Elsevier
Publishing Co., Inc., 1976), p. 152. See
also Don Peretz, "Energy Crisis: Israelis,
Arabs, and Iranians," The Energy Crisis and
U.S. Foreign Policy, p. 97.

157. The Arab countries that participated in the
cutback included: Saudi Arabia, Kuwait,
Libya, Algeria, Egypt, Syria, Ab Dhabi,
Bahrain, and Qatar. For the text of the
communique issued by the conference of the
Arab oil ministers, "announcing a gradual
reduction of oil production," see Middle East
Economic Survey (Beirut) 16 (19 October 1973):
iii-iv.

158. For the text of this announcement see Middle
East Economic Survey (Beirut) 17 (26 October
1973): 3.

159. Michael Tanzer, The Energy Crisis: World
Struggle for Power and Wealth (N.Y.: Monthly
Review Press, 1974), p. 128.

160. S.M. Miller, Roy Bennett, and Cyril Alapatt,
"Does the U.S. Economy Require Imperialism,"
in Robert J. Art and Robert Jervis, International Politics: Anarchy, Force, Imperialism
(Boston: Little, Brown and Company, 1973),
p. 357.

161. David Howard Davis, Energy Politics, (New York: St. Martin's Press, 1978), p. 92.

162. Ibid.

163. See Warren Christopher, Energy and Foreign Policy in Chau T. Phan, ed., World Politics, (Gilford: Dusking Publishing, 1980) p. 125.

164. Ibid.

165. Ibid.

166. For a review of the role of the oil companies in U.S. energy crisis see Ibid.

167. William B. Quandt, "Domestic Influences on United States Foreign Policy in the Middle East: The View from Washington," The Middle East: Quest for an American Policy, ed., Willard A. Beling (N.Y.: State University of New York Press, 1973), p. 280.

168. Ibid.

169. William B. Quandt, "United States Policy in the Middle East: Constraints and Choices," Political Dynamics in the Middle East, ed., Paul Y. Hammond and Sydney S. Alexander (N.Y.: American Elsevier Publishing Co., Inc., 1972), p. 529, n. 67.

170. Cited in Quandt, "U.S. Energy Policy," p. 283

171. For details see Bulloch, The Making of a War.

172. Kalb and Kalb, Kissinger, p. 484.

173. Quandt, "U.S. Energy Policy," p. 284.

174. Ibid.

175. Congressional Quarterly, Continuing Energy Crisis in America (Washington, D.C.: Congressional Quarterly, 1975), p. 30.

176. Ibid.

177. For analysis of the Israeli surprise, see
Avi Shlaim, "Failures in National Intelli-
gence Estimate: The Case of the Yom Kippur
War," World Politics 28 (April 1976); Amos
Perlmutter, "Israel's Fourth War, October
1973: Political and Military Misperception,"
Orbis 19 (Summer 1975): 434-460; Abraham
Ben-Zvi, "Misperceiving the Role of Perception:
A Critique," The Jerusalem Journal of Inter-
national Relations 2 (Winter 1976-1977): 74-
91; _____, "Hindsight and Foresight: A
Conceptual Framework for the Analysis of
Surprise Attacks," World Politics 28 (April
1976): 381-395; S.Z. Abramov, "The Agranat
Report and its Aftermath," Midstream 29
(June/July 1974): 16-28; Michael Handel,
Perception, Deception and Surprise: The Case
of the Yom Kippur War, Jerusalem Papers on
Peace Problems, no. 19. Also see Herzog,
The War of Atonement, pp. 40-55; The Insight
Team, The Yom Kippur War, pp. 90-113; and
Haim Var Lev, "Surprise in the Yom Kippur
War," Military Aspects of the Israeli-Arab
War, pp. 259-265.

178. Herzog, The War of Atonement, p. 41.

179. Cited in Shlaim, "Failures in National Intelligence," p. 362.

180. The Insight Team, The Yom Kippur War, p. 112;
Monroe and Farr-Hockley, The Arab-Israel War,
p. 18.

181. Heikal, The Road to Ramadan, p. 208.

182. For details see Bulloch, The Making of a War,
pp. 17-30.

183. Cited in Heikal, The Road to Ramadan, p. 208.

184. Laqueur, Confrontation, p. 46.

185. Heikal, The Road to Ramadan, p. 208.

About the Authors

Ray Maghroori received his Ph.D. in political science from the University of California, Riverside, in 1978. Dr. Maghroori has taught at the University of California, Santa Cruz, California State University at Long Beach, and San Bernardino Valley College. He is presently on the faculty of political science at the University of California, Riverside. Dr. Maghroori is co-editor of <u>International Relations' Third Debate: Globalism vs. Realism</u> (Boulder: Westview Press, 1982).

Stephen M. Gorman received his Ph.D. in political science from the University of California, Riverside, in 1977. He has taught at the State University of New York College at Fredonia, Dickinson College, and Purdue University. His recent publications include articles in the <u>Journal of Inter-American Studies and World Affairs</u>, <u>Inter-American Economic Affairs</u>, <u>Government and Opposition</u>, <u>Parameters: Journal of the US Army War College</u> and <u>Economic and Social Studies</u>. Dr. Gorman is on the political science faculty at North Texas State University.